God's Dream

Reflections on the Stations of the Cross
and
Selected Writings

Adelaide Wetherell Morley

Foreword by
Canon John Young

Other books by the same author:
A Hope and a Future: A Journey Out of the Depths
ISBN 1-904446-05-1

Published by AWM Publishing
© Adelaide W. Morley 2013

ISBN: 978-0-9575880-0-4

A CIP catalogue record for this book is available from the British Library

Printed In Great Britain by
Christian Book Printing (a trading name of Digital Print Media Ltd)

For Phil Hoar

Who has taught me and continues to teach me
so much about prayer.

and

For Diana Rance

A beloved friend, with whom I can be real

Contents

Foreword

This is not an 'easy read'. It is not a Twelve Step programme to peace and happiness. No, it is a gritty fourteen step tour to resurrection, via cruelty, suffering and death.

Adelaide's book holds up a mirror to the modern world by reflecting on Jesus' short journey from rigged trial to rugged cross. As she writes, she shines light into dark corners – and illuminates the personal journey which each of us must take.

But stick with it and you will find that suffering and death do not have the last word. No, that word is … Resurrection.

Her reflection on the Stations of the Cross, like the poems which follow, paint word pictures in dark colours. But the brightness and the light are made splendid because of the contrast.

These pages contain a moving personal testimony to Christian faith – a faith which sustains through tough times, and adds joy to happiness.

Thank you, Adelaide, for letting us share your journey.

John Young, York
January 2013

An Introduction and
A Few Words of Thanks

These writings are born out of my own times of prayer and meditation and via my own experience. As such, they are personal to me and sharing them in this way feels a bit scary: such sharing inevitably puts one in a vulnerable place. My request to you, as the reader, is to treat what you read with respect, take what is helpful and leave, without judging, what is not. If, as you read, something stirs in you, ask God to show you what the root of that stirring is – listen to God and to yourself.

Some of the writing in this book was written a number of years ago, others more recently. They are not in chronological order; I could not put them together in that way, even if asked. Over the years I have shared my writing with friends, many of whom have encouraged me to put what I have written together in a book, hence this book came into being.

The title of the book is from the poem, *God's Dream* on page 50.

I would like to thank all those who have inspired me to write, some of whom are mentioned in the book. I thank those who have encouraged me in my writing and encouraged me to put this book together, such as Olivia Taylor, whose usual emailed response to my sharing something I'd written has been, 'I hope you are keeping all these and putting them in a book' and Tim Stacey, who has asked on a number of occasions, if he could use what I had written in a church service that he would be leading.

I wrote the *Monologue: John the Baptist* and the poem, *The Path to God*, after walking through 'Stations of the Nativity', created by some of the students attending the 2012/13 SPIDIR Course at Wydale Hall, Yorkshire. I thank them and Fr. Antony Pritchett of Pickering Parish Church for his input into the content of the Station focusing on John the Baptist.

I thank Diana Rance for proof reading drafts of this book. I also thank her for her caring friendship over the years; I am grateful for her gifts of listening, encouragement and laughter. I dedicate this book to her.

I thank Phil Hoar, to whom I also dedicate this book, for his caring, insightful friendship, for listening and for teaching me so much about prayer and about God.

I thank John and Isabel Young for their encouragement, especially regarding *The Way of the Cross*. Thanks too to John, for agreeing to read through the draft copy and to write a foreword. I also thank Carrie Geddes for her advice and Mark Comer for helping with the design and layout of the book, a donation for which has been given to Christian Aid.

All the proceeds from the sale of this publication will be given to charity, including **Bungoma Calling** and **ActionAid**.

I also thank *Christian Book Printing* for all their help and advice and for printing this book.

And finally but by no means least, I thank Jonathan, my husband, for always being there.

Adelaide Morley
October 2013

'For God so loved the world
that he gave his one and only Son,
that whoever believes in him shall not perish
but have eternal life'
(John 3:16)

Your attitude should be the same as that of Christ Jesus:

Who, being in very nature God
did not consider equality with God
something to be grasped,
but made himself nothing,
taking the very nature of a servant,
being made in human likeness.
And being found in appearance as a man,
He humbled himself
and became obedient to
death – even death on a cross!
Therefore God exalted him to the
highest place
and gave him the name that is above
every name,
that at the name of Jesus every knee
should bow,
in heaven and on earth and under the earth,
and every tongue confess that
Jesus Christ is Lord,
To the glory of God the Father.
(Philippians 2:5-11)

The Way of the Cross

Reflections
On
The Stations of the Cross

1st Station: Jesus Before Pilate

Matthew 27:11-26

Jesus stands before Pilate accused. Pilate finds no cause for trial or punishment and states this. In John's gospel, Pilate says that he has the power to release Jesus and the power to crucify him. Yet, when he finds Jesus innocent, he forfeits his power and allows himself to be ruled by the crowd and his fears of losing his position.

Jesus is silent.

Knowing that Jesus has done no wrong, Pilate hands the innocent Jesus over to death: a gruelling and cruel death. Pilate simply declares himself innocent of Jesus' blood by washing his hands. He has Jesus flogged then hands him over to be crucified.

Innocent people continue to be accused and sentenced to imprisonment, or worse, today. Who are the innocent, yet accused today? They are the prisoners who have committed no crime but are imprisoned because of what they believe, because of the colour of their skin, their sexual orientation or their political beliefs. They are the abused child, wife, husband or elderly parent. They are those sentenced to unsafe working conditions, unfair wages, dirty water for drinking, not enough food to eat, those denied basic human rights: these are the innocent who are sentenced today.

And there are so many more.

Jesus stood alone in silence. His companions had left him, or stood far off, not wanting to be associated with him. Those he came to show the love of God to, shouted for his execution. No one spoke up for him, not even those who knew he had done no wrong.

Thinking about the innocent who are accused today, where do you stand? Do you stand with the crowd shouting "Crucify!"? Do you stand with Pilate saying, "I wash my hands; I am not to blame."? Or do you stand alongside the accused, supporting, encouraging and fighting for justice?

All humanity bears the heart of God within. When we touch the life of another, for good or ill, we touch the heart of God.

Jesus stood in silence waiting for Pilate's response, Jesus waits for our response too.

Prayer

Lord Jesus, you were innocent, yet accused and sentenced;
no-one spoke for you. There are many in our world today,
who are also innocent, yet are unjustly imprisoned in prison,
or in lives of abuse, oppression or want.
Forgive me for not speaking out against the injustices I see.
Forgive me for unjustly pointing the finger of accusation,
either out of fear or misunderstanding.
Show me my role in freeing the innocent and give me the courage
to stand alongside; show me Your way Jesus.
In Your name I pray. Amen.

Action

- *Find out about those imprisoned even though they have not committed a crime*

- *Inform yourself about abuse in the home*

- *Buy something with a fair-trade logo on it which you have not bought before and learn about where it has come from*

And...

- *Reflect on and pray about what you learn.*

2nd Station: Jesus Carries His Cross

John 19:17

Jesus carried his cross to the place of execution. Sometime before, Jesus had said to his followers that they should take up their cross (Matthew 10:38). He added, "One who wants to benefit from his life will lose it; one who loses his life for my sake will find it."

When people talk about 'the cross we bear', they are invariably talking about illness, a difficult relationship or some other problem area in their lives. But is that what Jesus meant when he said, "Take up your cross"?

Jesus often alluded to his innocent death – he knew that he had upset people in high places and that the authorities were out to trap him. For him, his life was a journey to the cross, whether he realised that at first or not.

What had Jesus' pathway to the cross been? It had been a life of love, self-giving, obedience to and trust in his heavenly Father. Yet, he was not neglectful of his own needs – he took rest, ate, enjoyed conversation, celebrations, went to weddings and festivals. He also took time aside to reflect and pray.

There were difficult times too – one only has to look at Gethsemane to see that; he also knew the grief of the death of a friend, rejection, being let down by his friends, being misunderstood and opposed, yet, in all that, he stood firm in his obedience and trust. He was always true to himself and his Father.

Jesus carried his cross, which led to his crucifixion, the way to which was a life of self-giving love. Jesus invites us to take up our cross too, to live Jesus' way of love and trust, even in the difficult times, and in doing so, to become more fully ourselves, as we move deeper into relationship with Him and become more fully alive.

Prayer

> Lord Jesus, I take up my cross and follow you.
> Enable me, by your Spirit, to live your life of love;
> help me to be faithful in my relationship with you.
> And when I grow weary, or when things get tough
> and I want to put down my cross, give me the strength
> I need to carry on.
> In Your Holy Name I pray. Amen.

Action

- *Reflect on what 'carrying your cross' has meant thus far for you*
- *Visit someone, or send a card to someone, you know to be in need*
- *Take time aside and try to pray in a new way: using the imagination, Lectio Divina or another way you have not tried before*

And

- *Reflect on and pray about what you learn.*

3rd Station: Jesus Falls for the First Time

Isaiah 53: 1-3

Taking the cross onto his abused body, Jesus not only takes on the weight of the wood, but the enormity of the situation falls on him too.

He staggers under the physical weight of the cross and the psychological and emotional weight of what is to come: a painful, humiliating and cruel death. His already torn body smarts at the weight that it is now being forced to bear.

In his weakened and broken body, we see the humanity of Jesus writ large: The man who is God hurts; the man who is God bleeds; the man who is God stumbles; the man who is God finds that his weakness is overwhelming and he falls into the dust. The weight of the cross pins him to the ground, as does the mental and emotional weight of the situation.

God falls.

God falls and, because of that, we can come to him when we fall. No longer do we have to hide ourselves away in shame or fear with a feeling of failure. Jesus understands our weakness and our falling. He knows what it is to be overwhelmed by the burden of a hopeless situation. He knows what it is to face fearful events head on and to feel crushed by those events. He knows what it is to fall into the dust.

Everyone 'falls' at some point in their lives: broken relationships, loss of a job, illness, grief... Different things affect different people in different ways; what makes one person fall, may not affect another; some find it difficult to get up again, others dust themselves off and carry on. Whatever the cause of the fall, however we react to it, we'd do well to remember that Jesus fell too, God fell, he sees and understands our falling and waits for us to stretch out our hand and take his as he gently helps us to stand again.

Prayer

> Lord Jesus, I bring before you those I know who today are
> feeling fearful, people who feel burdened by life's road.
> I bring to you those things that cause me to feel weak and helpless...
> By your Spirit, enable them, and me, to keep going,
> keep living and to keep hoping, bring us through,
> that we might once again stand.
> To the glory of God the Father. Amen.

Action

- *Reflect on the ways that God has brought you through difficult times and thank him for it*

- *Show God's love to someone who is struggling with a difficult situation*

- *Give an hour or two of your time to help in a charity shop or another charity outlet*

And

- *Reflect on and pray about what you learn.*

4th Station: Jesus Meets His Mother
Luke 2:34-35

"My son, what have they done to you?" That was all I said. I reached out to touch his blood streaked face; I wanted to say so much more, many thoughts crowded my mind but none coherent. The pain in my chest was piercing as I took in the sight of him.

Sharp thorns, from the mock crown they'd put on him, cut into his head; his body was bruised, his skin ripped.

My strong, beautiful boy looked so weak and helpless and I could do nothing to ease his pain.

"Don't worry, mama," he gasped. Then he was gone: pushed forwards, ordered to go on – we'd had but a few precious moments.

I turned to watch him, then began to follow. How could I leave my boy? As I walked, memories and questions flooded my mind. I remembered when he was a little boy, always asking questions, always ready to help, to learn – that time we found him in the temple, how afraid I was then. So inquisitive and exasperating at times too. But my boy.

Angels sang at his birth; kings and shepherds visited – I marvelled but didn't understand, not really, I'm still not sure I do yet.

As I followed, a soldier prodded and I wanted to push him away, tell him to leave my boy alone; tell them all to go; I wanted to hold my son once more in my arms, tell him all would be well again, but it was hopeless, I could do nothing.

Thoughts crowded in again. Oh, why didn't he listen to us? Why didn't he come that day when we went to him? We knew even then that he was putting himself in danger but he wouldn't come, just said that his mother and brothers were those who heard God's word. I was so hurt, yet my heart ached with fear for him.

When that happened I remembered the words of old Simeon when he spoke at Jesus' dedication and talked about a sword piercing my heart. I thought that had been when his brothers and I went to speak to him one day; the place was so crowded, we had to ask someone to tell Jesus we were there. On hearing that we waited for him, he asked 'Who is my mother and who are my brothers?' then he pointed to his followers and said they were. But no, that hurt but this is the sword old Simeon talked about: the murder of my son. A sword through the heart is certain death and any mother who loses a child in death, however violent or peaceful that death, dies a little herself too.

That's how it felt, that a part of me was dying, as I saw my boy, torn and bruised, carrying that cross to his death.

Prayer

Loving God, please be with all mothers and fathers the world over.
Give them wisdom, integrity and, most of all,
love, in their parenting.
Be with parents and guardians, who struggle to ease the pain of their children when they are ill or in distress; be with those who struggle to provide even the most basic things like food, water, education or a home, for their children and be with those who grieve the loss of a child.
Show me where I can support and share with parents who cross my path, that I may bring comfort, encouragement,
care and love, in Jesus' name. Amen

Action

- *Reflect on your own upbringing, who were the people most important to you, who influenced you, who encouraged you? What would you like to say to them?*

- *If you have the opportunity this week, encourage a child for who they are (rather than what they do)*

- *Pray for parents, especially those who struggle in their parenting and for young parents*

And

- *Reflect on and pray about what you learn.*

5th Station: Simon of Cyrene
Matthew 27:32

I thought that I was in the wrong place at the wrong time, when the soldier singled me out to help carry the cross of a condemned man. I was soon to learn otherwise.

Tired from my day's work in the fields, I asked the soldier, "Why me?"

"Shut up and get on with it, before we give you one of your own!" the soldier shouted in reply whilst raising his whip.

I quickly did as I was told.

The man whose cross it was, was in a terrible state – skin torn to shreds, blood everywhere, yet, he looked at me with eyes of compassion, eyes that said, "Sorry", even a glimmer of a warm smile rose on his lips.

I felt uneasy at this 'welcome'. He, seeing my reluctance, continued to carry the greater load. "What have you done anyway?" I asked harshly, not wanting to seem friendly.

He spoke in short gasps, "I proclaimed... good news... to the poor... made the... blind see... healed the sick... taught about... the... Kingdom of God. Every word was an effort. He struggled to speak again. "Some... didn't like... what... I said... They were expecting... something... someone... else."

"So what did they want, if not someone who heals those who are sick and speaks of God's work?" I thought that he must be deluded; the pain had obviously affected his mind.

"They wanted... a... warrior," he replied, "they wanted..."

"Silence!" shouted the soldier as his whip hissed through the air.

At the same time the prisoner fell, the cross with him. He lifted his head, half blinded by the blood and sweat streaking his face. Then a woman ran forward, "Jesus," she said, that was all, then she wiped his face. Then, for a moment, they looked at each other – there was such love in that gaze; everything was said in the silence of that gaze.

The soldier pushed the woman aside, out of the way, but her eyes never left her Jesus.

I saw the whip being raised again and rushed forward, helping Jesus to his feet. His blood and sweat mingled with my own sweat but it did not matter. He bent to take up the cross again, "No", I said, "you've carried it far enough, I'll take it." Taking the whole of its weight, I urged him to walk ahead.

"Thank you," he said in an exhausted whisper.

He thanked me. Me, who carried the instrument of his execution to the place of its use.

Prayer

> Lord, although reluctant, Simon served you in helping to
> carry the cross, please show me where I can serve you too.
> Help me to be willing and ready.
> Open my heart to share your love with those around me,
> in whatever way I can.
> Be with those who are struggling to serve you at the moment
> and those who are persecuted for doing so.
> Protect us and keep us safe. In your Holy Name. Amen.

Action

- *Reflect on how you have served the Lord this past week*
- *Find out about Christians who are persecuted in the world today*
- *Send a card of encouragement to someone struggling in their faith*

And

- *Reflect on and pray about what you learn*

6th Station: Veronica Wipes Jesus' Face

Isaiah 53:4-6

As he walked towards Golgotha, streaked with blood from the flogging he had endured, in his weakened state, staggering under the weight of the cross, there would have been those who jeered, as some do outside court rooms today. There will have also been many who turned their faces and shielded the eyes of their children from the sceptical before them.

Yet, there was one, Veronica, who was reputed to have moved forwards, towards Jesus and, in a beautiful act of love, wiped his blood streaked, sweating face, wiping the blinding moisture from his eyes.

She saw his need and acted, others saw and turned away, even those who had been closest to him kept their distance.

Given the enormity of his pain and suffering, one may wonder, 'What was the point of wiping his face?' Surely, it would have been a drop in the ocean given the amount of relief he must have needed? Nevertheless, we need to remember that the ocean is made up of drops. This act of love may have been an oasis in the desert of Jesus' pain.

There are many who are in pain today: emotional, physical, mental and spiritual. When we ask who the 'Veronicas' are today, we might think of the late Mother Theresa as one, or religious leaders, or others who work tirelessly for the poor, the sick, the unloved and rejected, and yes, each will have been Veronica to many but each one of us can be a 'Veronica' too, to those whom we know who are in pain and need. A card, a phone call, a gentle touch, or companionable silence, may not seem or feel much in themselves but each can become an oasis in a desert of pain, grief or struggle and it may just be the thing that gets the person through.

The cloth Veronica used to wipe Jesus' face, is said to have come away with an imprint of his face on it. Being 'Veronica' to another leaves a similar impression, for not only is the one who is helping changed, but the one who has helped is also changed.

Prayer

Loving, merciful Lord, I thank you for those who have been
Veronica to me in my times of pain and distress.
Show me, Lord, where and how I can be Veronica to others.
I pray in the precious name of Jesus, my Lord. Amen.

Action

- *Notice this week those who are as Veronica to you and thank God for them*
- *Be aware of God's promptings for you to be Veronica to others*
- *Reflect on how, or if, those being as Veronica to you, and you to others, has changed you*

And...

- *Reflect on and pray about what you learn*

7th Station: Jesus Falls a Second Time

Psalm 22:6-17

Having witnessed the grief and pain of his mother and experienced the tenderness of Veronica, Jesus falls for a second time.

One wonders which was most burdensome for him: what was most difficult to bear?

Was it the beatings, torn flesh, the weakening of the body? Was it the Cross itself? Was it the desertion of his beloved friends? The broken heart of his mother or the loving touch of Veronica in a world turned to and full of anger, pain and madness? Maybe it was all these things and more.

Previously, before his arrest, so many had flocked to him seeking his help, his touch, his counsel, his truth, yet, it seems that few openly grieved for him in his humiliation and need while many cried "crucify!"

The weight of his grief must have been tremendous, little wonder he fell.

There are many in our world today who also experience heart wrenching grief. Often friends fall away because they have no words, feel afraid, or don't know how to respond to
the childless couple who long for a child,
the grieving person, whose partner or friend has died,
a broken marriage,
a wayward son or daughter,
the birth of a child, who has special needs,
redundancy,
the death of a teenager…
and so the list goes on…

Many fall away when faced with such things, not knowing how to react or what to say and not realising that those who do stay are also afraid, also struggle, also don't know what to say. They stay, even in their feeling of inadequacy, not always knowing that their presence, even their silent presence, is enough.

Prayer

Father God, help me to stay alongside those I know who are grieving; show me when it is time to give them space.
When it is time to speak, please give me the words to say.
When it is time to be silent, let me know it in my spirit and not be uncomfortable with it.

Teach me to listen, to have patience and help me not to be afraid. Enable me, Lord God, to help them to stand again, to laugh again, once the grief has eased. Help me to remember that grief is a precious thing, fragile, unpredictable and in need of expression. Help me to give a safe place to those who grieve. Amen.

Action

- *Think about the grief you have experienced in your life and what/who helped you through it and why*
- *Find out about grief patterns and how grief affects individuals*
- *As far as you can, be alongside someone you know who has suffered a loss – that is, if they want you to*

And...

- *Reflect on and pray about what you learn.*

8th Station: Weeping Daughters of Jerusalem

Luke 23:27-31

Given the customs of the time, the women crying a lament for Jesus, may well have been professional mourners. They may not have realised who their lament was for. To them, he may simply have been another man, a convicted man, going to his death.

Jesus' own lament for Jerusalem, born in his words to the women, is reminiscent of his tears for her (Luke 19:44). Tears shed as he approached Jerusalem, in that throng of celebration and worship we now call, "The Triumphal Entry". Then, Jesus wept for the city and her people, here he echoes that lament.

Jesus wept because of, and lamented, the blindness of Jerusalem and her children, which, he knew, would lead to her downfall. He longed for her to see him for who he really was: the long awaited Messiah. He longed for her children to recognise in him God's mercy, love and grace but they were blind to this and it broke his heart. Even on the way to his own death he lamented the lost, he longed for them to see differently, to see what he saw but they remained blind to God's revelation of himself in Jesus.

God continues to reveal himself in the world today: through his word, the touch of a loving friend, through his creation and in many other ways. He longs for his children to respond to him, mourning each lack of response but never giving up and delighting in each individual that does respond, each time they respond to his call. For God is a jealous God, not jealous of, but jealous for: jealous for each of his precious children to see him for who he is, to know his love and, in him, to know life.

Prayer

Lord, help me today to see differently.
Help me to see you in the many ways you choose
to reveal yourself to me.
Uncover my blindness, work with me to take down the blinds
I have drawn around myself and let me see the gifts of love,
grace and mercy that you gift to me and all people.
Open my eyes, Lord, that I might see anew and reach out to others
with the love, peace, mercy and grace that you share with me.
In Jesus' name. Amen.

Action

- *Reflect on the ways that God has spoken to you in the past*
- *Ask yourself what stops you seeing and hearing what God wishes to share with you*
- *Give to someone a little of what God has given to you today*

And...

- *Reflect on and pray about what you learn*

9th Station: Jesus Falls a Third Time

Psalm 42:9-10

Jesus' broken, bleeding body crashes to the floor and, for the third time, his face is in the dust.

His legs and arms are weakened by the shear effort of making that pain-filled walk, whilst carrying that heavy cross. Each jolt of the cross sending electric shocks of pain throughout his body. Falling, though painful, would have given momentary relief from his physical burden. He may have felt like he couldn't go on, not even feeling that he had the strength to stand again.

Somehow, however, he struggled to use his pain-filled arms and legs to pull himself up again, taking the cross again and continuing the painful, piteous walk to his death.

Jesus' struggle is beyond our imagining but all of us have our own struggles in life. Each of us will at some time feel overwhelmed and there may have been times, or may be times now, when we have felt like we cannot go on any longer.

Those on the Christian journey are not immune to such times. Some have said of their life with Christ, "It would be so much easier just to give up and walk away." This might be so, Jesus, after all, does show us that following him is not easy; he taught his disciples, and teaches us, that His road is a road of joy and life but also of struggle and hardship: not necessarily material hardship.

There are times of 'drought', when it feels like God has withdrawn his Spirit, times of doubt when it seems that belief in God is nonsense. There may be times of persecution, struggle with temptation or utter despair, as we call with the Psalmist, "Where are you God? Why have you forgotten me?"

Yes, the road is hard and sometimes we never find a reason why; there may be times when we feel like giving up and going our own way; there will be times when we fall into the dust and not want to get up again.

Jesus did find the strength to stand again, and the strength to continue that long walk of the cross. He will also give us the strength to stand again when we fall too. We just have to ask and wait for his response. It is not always an easy wait; it is not always easy to agree to continue but it is worth the effort in the end.

The journey doesn't end with the falling; it ends when we decide not to get up again.

Prayer

> Father God, help me to keep going when I want to give up.
> Help me to stand again when I fall.
> Help me to accept your gift of grace,
> and ever remind me of your promise that you will
> always be with me,
> In Jesus' name I pray. Amen.

Action

- *Reflect on the times you have 'fallen' in your Christian life and what/who helped you to stand again*
- *Share with a trusted friend how the Lord has helped you in difficult times*
- *Write a Psalm to the Lord about your experiences*

And…

- *Reflect on and pray about what you learn*

10th Station: Jesus is Stripped, Abused and Humiliated

Mark 15:15-20a

The taunting, name calling, humiliating and hitting of Jesus by the soldiers is akin to playground bullies, writ large. Shockingly such dehumanizing behaviour towards prisoners still goes on in the world today, in similar forms of unjust and humiliating torture. It is also the case that individuals and groups continue to be abused because of their faith.

There are people in positions of authority and power who abuse that power: employers with employees, teachers who humiliate children in the classroom and parents who do the same at home.

Although we may not taunt and abuse on the scale seen in this text, and we might shake our heads at abusive employers, parents and teachers, we are all capable of undermining and hurting those around us.

Lashing out with the tongue in anger can cut to the heart. Malicious gossip abuses the subject of that gossip and encourages others to do the same.

What is it that causes individuals, groups and even we ourselves to react so negatively against another?

Often, there are a number of reasons. If one feels threatened by, or fearful of, difference, or feels a lack of control in a situation, one may react negatively; prejudice, that is, a lack of understanding of the other, may result in humiliating malicious behaviour or words towards the other person. Fear, in its many guises, is a big motivator for abuse. One may judge a person by their dress, behaviour, creed, colour, sexual orientation or some other aspect of themselves or their lives, without really knowing or speaking to the individual to discover who they really are, to try to understand their point of view.

If faced with negative feelings about another it may be helpful to step back and ask, "Why do I feel this way?"

The soldiers taunted and tortured Jesus because they had the power to do so and they didn't understand who he was. We have the power to hurt with our actions and words too. Sometimes in our frustrations and fear it is not easy to control our tongue, it may help to remember Jesus' words, "...whenever you did this to these little ones who are my brothers and sister, you did it to me." (Matthew 25:40). There may be times when we do lash out, in our fears, in our anxiety, because of the stresses of life, whatever the reason, we can also know that Jesus will welcome us back to him and forgive, comfort and heal us.

Prayer

Lord Jesus, I am often too quick to judge,
too quick to lash out with my tongue. I am truly sorry.
Give me a heart of grace and compassion,
Lord. Help me not to be afraid of difference and to remember
that you are in control. Help me to love, rather than to condemn,
to build up, rather than to knock down and help me always to
remember, Lord, that when I interact with others,
I interact with you. In your name I pray. Amen.

Action

- *Reflect on the last time you hurt someone because of what you said or did and ask God to show you what was behind your words/actions. If you feel able to, talk to the individual about it*

- *Find out about prisoners who are tortured today, pray for them and write to your MP with your concerns*

- *Talk to someone who has hurt you in the past about that hurt and try to get an understanding of what was going on for them*

And...

- *Reflect on and pray about what you learn*

11th Station: Jesus is Crucified

Matthew 27:33-44

Jesus is forced onto his torn back, nails hammered into his wrists and feet. The wood and nails of his trade, and his father's before him, become the instruments of his death.

As he is lifted, nailed to the cross, the weight of his body strains on his arms and his chest feels like it might burst, as he gasps for breath.

Then soldiers gamble for and share out, his clothes as they wait for him to die: This is the King of the Jews, the Chosen One, the Messiah.

"This is Jesus, The King of the Jews", reads the sign above him. Many had believed it, many had trusted in him, saw him as the long awaited and mighty Messiah but now here he was, crucified with common criminals. All hope lost.

Grief and disappointment manifest themselves in insults and sneers, while those eager to see his downfall call similar insults and scoff at him to reveal himself as the promised King, that they might believe. But that's not how faith works.

The people and the teachers and leaders of the law who scoffed, had their own ideas of God and the promised Messiah and of their rolls in God's plan. Jesus didn't fulfil the picture they'd made for themselves of the promised Messiah and he threatened their positions, their traditions, and their very beliefs: he didn't fit, so he was labelled an imposter and sentenced to death.

Jesus' true title was written on the sign above him on the cross but it was used and placed there both as an insult and as a challenge against him.

Jesus wasn't what the people expected of God. God continues to be a God whose thoughts and actions are beyond our understanding and expectations. How often then, do we point the finger to the unexpected, to those who show their faith in ways different to us and scoff, saying, "Ah, this is not God!"?

Prayer

Holy Father God, your whole is unknowable;
forgive me when I think I have you figured out.

Holy Father God, You are uncontainable,
forgive me when I try to put you in a box and restrict you.
Holy Father God, You reveal yourself in many ways,
some I fail to know, acknowledge or understand.
Help me, by your Spirit, to be ever open to you
and the different ways you show yourself to me.
Help me to be ever open to your surprising revelations,
ever open and ready to receive all you offer,
even if at first it seems strange to me.
Let me not crucify your revelation of yourself in and through me.
In Jesus name. Amen.

Action

- *Attend worship at a denomination not your own and experience a different style of worship*

- *Reflect on the many ways that God has spoken to you and share what you find with someone else*

- *Imagine that you are at Jesus' crucifixion, listen to the accusations of those around you, notice how you feel and what your reaction is to the situation*

And...

- *Reflect on and pray about what you learn*

12th Station: Jesus Dies

Matthew 27:45-54

'Eloi, Eloi, lama sabachthani?' 'My God, my God, why have you forsaken me?' Jesus cried out at the moment of greatest despair, the terrible moment that he felt separation from his Father and himself.

Even at this time of crisis for Jesus, his tormentors hoped for a miracle – for Elijah to appear and save Jesus from certain death, if that would happen they would believe.

There was a miracle that day, but most of the people passed by disappointed, missing its significance. Only the centurion recognised its truth.

Jesus called out in agony, 'Why have you abandoned me, Father?' As far as we know, he got no reply. Yet, even out of that feeling of abandonment, Jesus called again to his Father, "Into your hands I commit my spirit" (Luke 23:46) and in doing so, he breathed his last and died.

Even in the place of abandonment Jesus knew that the only place for him, the place where he most desired to be, was with his Father in Heaven. His faith and trust carried him through his feelings of overwhelming grief, loss and abandonment.

Have you yourself known that feeling of being abandoned by God? Have you known that feeling of doubting God's love for you, or, indeed, his very existence?

Jesus called out in despair and agony; we can do the same, crying out to God, "Why have you forsaken me?" "Why have you abandoned me?" Jesus cried in honesty; he was honest about where he was, how he felt, the way things were from his perspective and we are called to do the same, to remove the smiling masks and be Real before God. If, like Jesus, in your grief you continue to trust and have faith, hanging onto God through it all, knowing he holds on to you, then, like the centurion, others might look at us and say, 'Truly, he/she is a child of God.'

Prayer

Father God, when you seem far away, when my faith and strength are weak, when life's storms threaten to overwhelm, enable me,

by your Spirit, to continue to trust, to continue to have faith in You, even in the feeling of emptiness, loneliness, pain and grief, help me, like Jesus, to continue to commit my life to you.
In Jesus name. Amen.

Action

- *Remember times when you have felt God really close and write these down in a journal. Re-read these when God seems far away*

- *Share with someone any doubts you have experienced or are experiencing, it may be helpful for your both*

- *Note in your Bible, or in a notebook or journal, verses of scripture that you find inspiring, comforting or which help you to express how you feel (Jesus called out from the cross using Ps 22.). Use these when you need to*

And...

- *Reflect on and pray about what you learn*

13th Station: Jesus' Body is Taken Down From the Cross

John 19:38-40

Joseph of Arimathea.

It was I who went to Pilate and asked to take Jesus' body down from the cross. Pilate didn't believe Jesus was already dead; he had to ask a centurion to check. I waited in stony silence, sickened by what had happened, I couldn't bear being in Pilate's presence.

I guess I was sickened by my own actions too or, should I say, lack of action? Yes, like Pilate I'd pointed out that Jesus was innocent of any crime and didn't deserve death, especially one as cruel as the Roman cross. But I was shouted down and I was too afraid to speak again.

That's been my problem – fear – I've watched Jesus these past years, heard stories about him, listened to him, seen evidence of his miracles; I've studied the scriptures and longed in my heart for God's Kingdom. I believed this Jesus... I saw, in all he did and said, the Kingdom I've so longed for.

Yet, I kept on the periphery, worried about what others might think, never able to take that final stop to follow him; I mean, I'm a prominent member of the council, it's an important, privileged role, surely you understand, I couldn't give that up... well, that's what I thought; that's how I felt... but things change.

It may have been too late for Jesus but the time had come for me to be open, honest about what I felt, if only to myself.

I had done nothing for Jesus during his life, except accept in my secret heart his truth. He hadn't known that; now he is dead and never will... What good is such truth if it is kept a secret? Now my heart aches with what might have been... Now I want to reveal what I've kept hidden for so long, burning inside... I could keep silent no longer.

Hence I went to Pilate.

Eventually word came, yes, Jesus was dead, just as I said he was. Pilate gladly gave him over to me: couldn't wait to get rid of him.

I wasn't the only one on the Council who felt what had happened, and the Council's and Pilate's part in it, was wrong. Nicodemus thought so too and he came to help take Jesus' body down from the cross.

Neither of us thought about the laws of cleanliness and death. We didn't leave the taking down of Jesus' body to others, we couldn't... we touched him, held him, pulled out the blood soaked nails and lowered his heavy, lifeless body down ourselves... He was unrecognisable: skin torn, sweat, blood... All was silence. Grief was palpable.

We carried him to my own tomb – the only thing I ever gave to him: a grave.

We did what we could, followed the customs using spices of myrrh and aloes and wrapped him in linen cloths...

When we'd finished we pushed a large, heavy stone in front of the cave – they'd done enough, they weren't going to do any more.

I did nothing for him in life and the shame of this hit me again, when I saw those women, those who had done so much for him, watching from a distance...

Nicodemus told me that he'd spoken to Jesus once and Jesus talked to him about rebirth – the need to be reborn... I wished I could be reborn, not feel the shame, the hurt, the lie I'd lived...

I find myself wondering, if Jesus came again, now, would I act differently? Would you?

Prayer

> Merciful Father, forgive the times I have been silent
> when I could have spoken out for you.
> Forgive the times I have put my reputation before my following of you.
> Forgive the times I have acted in fear rather than out of your love.
> Help me, Father, to be open about my love for you, to myself, to
> others and to you.
> In Jesus' name. Amen.

Action

- *Write a love letter to God*
- *Tell someone who doesn't know about your faith what it means to you*
- *Ask God to help you work through one thing that stops you getting closer to him*

And...

- *Reflect on and pray about what you learn*

14th Station: Jesus' Body is Laid in the Tomb

John 19:41-42

Jesus is laid in a tomb: hurriedly buried by a once secret follower.

It is his disciples and followers who feel abandoned now. Jesus is dead. Separation complete. Hope lost.

The one they believed would save them, the one they named, 'Messiah' and 'Lord' is laid and sealed in a tomb. Dead.

No ceremony. No fuss. Just, gone.

All they had believed in, shattered. Confusion and fear fill their hearts and minds.

They thought that He, Jesus, was the One – hadn't God the Father spoken to their hearts that this was so?

"You are the Christ", Peter had said, "Man hasn't told you this, "Jesus replied, "It is from above."

So, what now?

How could they trust their feelings, their thoughts, or their beliefs again?

The ground they thought to be sure and firm has suddenly opened up and caused them to fall into uncertainty.

So, what do they do?

They go back to what they know to be real. They keep the Sabbath and later, go fishing.

Their despair is not unique. There may be times when you have believed that God has spoken or times when he seems to have shown a way forward which seems to lead nowhere.

There may have been, or may be now times, when it seems all you believe in is challenged and you're not certain of anything anymore, not even God.

At such times as this, it may be wise to 'go back to what you know' – to remember when you know that God has touched your life and in that remembering wait in the uncertainty and confusion with God and for God.

The first followers of Jesus had to wait for their confusion and sense of hopelessness to change and it was a gradual revelation. It is the same for Jesus' followers today.

God doesn't leave us abandoned and confused in hopelessness, he gives new insights, new understanding of himself, ourselves and others but it can be very gradual as he gently leads.

Yes, there can also be times when there is no answer, or the answer we are given is confusing in itself, but, if we are open, even then God gives us new insight into His Mysterious Majesty, his unknowableness. Even in the unknowing, he leads us closer to himself.

Prayer

Father, sometimes it feels as though all I have been certain of has come crashing down around my feet and I find that I can no longer trust the voice I thought to be yours.
At these times, Father, keep me faithful. Be with me in my waiting, until the confusion has dawned into new enlightenment.
And when it seems that there is no answer,
or the answer itself is confusing, help me,
even in my unknowing, to grow deeper in love with you.
In Jesus' name. Amen.

Action

- *Write a letter to someone (not necessarily to send) telling them of your experience of God and what that means to you*

- *Reflect on a time when you faced confusion in your faith journey, or were seeking answers that were not forthcoming, and write about it in a journal/diary*

- *Imagine yourself at the tomb where Jesus was laid, spend some time there, notice how you feel and what thoughts come to mind, then spend some time reflecting on it*

And...

- *Reflect on and pray about what you learn*

On The 15th Station

The Way of the Cross or Stations of the Cross, journey through Jesus' last steps, from his trial to his death on the cross and, finally, his burial.

Traditionally, there have been fourteen Stations, however, in recent years many have added a 15th Station: The Resurrection, reminding those who walk The Way of the Cross, that the death of Christ is not the end of the story. When I first wrote these reflections on the Stations of the Cross, I chose to be true to the traditional 14 Stations, making room for the emptiness and silence of Holy Saturday (sometimes known as silent Saturday) and leaving the 15th Station, the Resurrection, for Easter Day.

However, for anyone wishing to continue along the journey and wishing to incorporate a 15th Station, please feel free to do so by turning to the monologue with the voice of Mary Magdalene at the resurrection, on page 136 or the monologue of the disciple on the road to Emmaus, on page 138.

Spend some time pondering on what strikes you and what God might be saying. Then, over the following days, ask the Holy Spirit to show you signs of resurrection in your own life and the lives and situations around you. Ask God to show you where you can bring his Resurrection Light into the world.

Selected Poems

God's Dream

'I dreamed a dream,' said God,
'And you were born.
I weaved your every cell together,
Each with the thread of my love.

'I chose you as mine from the start,
Wrote your days in my big book;
I sing and dance when you smile
And hold you to my heart when you cry.

'You are my beloved, my joy,
Why then so sad, so full of sorrow?'
'I am wonderfully made,' said I,
'And I marvel at your grace and love.

'Yet, I am not the dream you dreamed,
I am spoiled within and without;
Sin has changed me – my own and others':
I am not the dream you bore.'

'Ah, my child, my love, my joy,
My dream is the very core of you,
Woven into every cell, every part,
Nothing can shatter the dreams I dream.

'You are the dream I dreamed,
The rest can be washed away,
In gentle, patient time, you'll see,
I dreamed the dream that is you.'

'Let me see the dream you dreamed,' I said,
'Let me feel and let me know,
That your dream continues, alive in me
And will never die, will only grow.'

Love Holds Me

Love holds me
He calls softly
For me to come closer,

Love holds me,
Though in life's storms
I miss the sound of his voice,

Love holds me,
He sings a song of welcome
And dances with me in joy,

Love holds me,
When I feel lost and alone,
I am certain

Love holds me
And will never let go,
Love holds me.

The Desert's Song

Come to me and listen,
Hear the flower
Breaking through dry land,
Rejoicing in the Light,
Hear the scurrying lizard
Heading for cover
As you pass by.
See a palette of colour:
Sand, rock, bush, tree.
Feel my textures,
Coarse sand,
Wind smoothed rocks,
Sharp plants, rough trees,
Delicate leaves.

You compare yourself to me
When feeling
Dead, empty,
But look closer,
See my beauty,
Listen, hear my song,
Feel, touch my heart,

I am bursting with life,
Seen and unseen,
And so, my child, are you.

I Have Found My First Love

I have found my first love again,
He was right here,
I was lost and bereft,
He whispered to me gently.

I longed to hear his voice,
He sang me songs of love,
I searched for him everywhere,
He was always near.

I yearned for his touch,
He held and stroked me,
I was full of sorrow and confusion,
He guided me with compassion.

My frantic search was useless,
He was nowhere to be found,
In sorrow, I sat still and waited,
He smiled and opened his arms.

In my waiting, his presence dawned,
In my silence, I heard his song,
In my stillness, I felt his touch,
And I realised that he'd never gone.

(With thanks to Rita)

Rainbow Tears

Tears shot through with Light
Hold Rainbows,
Light enters and transforms:
Beauty from pain.

Tears of grief hold the
Promise, when
Transforming Light breaks through,
Birthing new hope.

So cry, cry your tears
Honestly,
Open pain to His Light,
Rainbows will come.

Abandoned

(Stations of the Cross: Jesus Dies)

Pain and grief overwhelm,
Where are you?
My body is torn,
My heart broken,
Where are you?
All hope is lost,
Where are you?
In anguish I cry out,
You are silent,
Where are you?
Death is here

I give myself to you,
I am yours.

No Words

No words.
No need for words.
You read my tears,
Like words.
Each one to you is
Precious.
You collect
And hold them
In your heart.

No words.
Only groans and longing.
Each you hear and
Hold still
Within your
Hands.
Giving space for
Freedom and
Expression.

No Words.
Yet much is said,
Through tears and groans
And longing.
Silently
You hold me,
And listen
As I speak with
No words.

No Room

No room.
No place to be born.
No home.
No comfortable crib.
Unwanted refugee: Jesus

Malicious whispers,
Trick questions,
Unjust judgments,
Seeking to break you
Unwanted healer: Jesus

Deserted, rejected.
Alone, Tried
Silent
Whipped
Crucified Lord: Jesus

Risen, glorified,
Waiting
No place to be born?
Be born in me, Jesus,
That I may be born in you.

Advent Candles

The first candle flickers
Dancing into life,
Lighting the darkness of the room,
Reminding of others' light
Lighting my way.

The second candle glows
God is all around,
Speaking his words of love and peace,
Encouraging, enabling,
Lighting my way.

The third candle stands tall,
Drawing me closer,
Revealing barriers and masks
Now highlighting ways forward,
Lighting my way.

The fourth candle warms:
Humble light, yet strong,
Fearful, questioning, puzzled,
Brings clarity, goes forward,
Lighting my way.

The final candle lit,
Bright as rising Sun,
God's Word spoken, lighting the world,
God's Word wooing me to come,
Lighting my way.

You Hold Me

Darkness falls,
Yet, you hold me
Turmoil roars within,
Yet, you hold me
You're so far away,
Yet, you hold me

I cry for you,
Yet, you hold me
Silence and emptiness prevail,
Yet, you hold me
Tears cascade,
Yet, you hold me
Empty, all is empty,
Yet, you hold me

Light dawns,
You hold me
Storms subside,
You hold me
Understanding flickers,
You hold me
Tears cease,
You hold me
Stillness quietens,
You hold me
I turn
You hold me
I know
You hold me.

I wrote the following poem while visiting my dear friends Nigel and Heather Fry, the name of their church was the inspiration. Heather died in 2011 and is sadly missed; Nigel continues to be Vicar of Christ the Carpenter Church, Dogsthorpe, Peterborough.

Christ The Carpenter

He chose me,
My protective exterior
Coarse and rough
In his hands, yet,
Lovingly he held me.

He stroked me
And thought silently,
Gently he began
To remove the hard
Outer layer I'd formed.

At first I complained,
Jarred his hands
As he worked,
Felt exposed, unprotected,
But his touch calmed me.

In my naked state
He dealt with greater care,
Removed rough, unnecessary unevenness,
Exposing a beauty
I hadn't realised was there.

Then came deep pain,
I felt he'd forgotten me,
Deep cuts, shapes,
Grooves made
Into my tender nakedness.

I cried out in despair,
My soft flesh wept,
Then, I looked and wondered
At what I saw:
Scars of pain, yet beauty.

He ran his hands over me,
Seeing with hands
Imperfections, gently
Rubbing them smooth,
Until all was ready.

The Carpenter smiled,
I was no longer afraid,
He covered me and
Together we marvelled
At the heart he'd revealed.

Unexpected Love

Weary of life's burdens
I long for death,
But the Lord comes
In gentleness;
I hide my face and weep
For what has been
And what is;
He silently holds me,
Knowing each tear:
The heartache, the pain;
He envelops me
Even in my grief,
And shows his love
In unexpected ways.

The Gift

I thought of buying flowers,
But they would fade and die,
And what you have given
Will last for all time.

I thought of buying chocolates,
Tasty, sweet, though not nutritious,
But what you have given
Is wholesome, life giving and good.

I thought of buying jewellery,
Which adorns the body,
But what you have given
Enriches the core of who we are.

I thought of buying an ornament,
A dog, or a cat to sit on a shelf,
But what you have given
Is alive and free, growing and learning.

Many things I have thought of buying
To reflect our thanks
For what you have given,
But nothing mirrors your gift to us.

Our greatest gift to you, I now know,
Is to take what you have given,
And live it each day,
All our lives through.

A Poem for Thelma

Thelma

Tirelessly you journey with me
Through the dark corridors of my life.
You provide a safety net
As I walk a tightrope of pain.

Hearing what I have to share,
And without taking control,
You encourage me on further,
Guiding my painful steps.

Even when I stumble or fall,
When I retrace my steps in fear,
Or in my pain turn on you
You remain near, supporting.

Laughter is your gift to me,
Sometimes embraced, taken and shared,
Sometimes rejected as I punish you
For pain you didn't cause.

My gift to you is a song of thanks,
Which flows from deep within my heart,
For although I see no journey's end,
You've born in me a hope for one.

As you walk along beside me,
Caring, encouraging, binding, loving,
See the freedom begin to grow,
And know your toil is not in vein.

The Holding Place

My heart is heavy with grief,
It is too painful to look back,
Too difficult to move forward,
God is holding me, waiting patiently,
In the holding place.

I feel I should move on,
Read, pray, write,
God knows I don't have the energy,
And holding me waits, in patience and love,
In the holding place.

At times my tears flow freely,
My heart feels it might tear in two,
God knows and respects the pain in those tears,
And patiently holds me, until the shakings cease,
In the holding place.

I'm in the holding place,
Where God holds on to me,
Feeling and sharing my pain and grief,
Patiently holding, lovingly caring,
In the holding place.

My Child

My dear child,
It is as if you've died
Before being born,
Before being conceived.

How I have longed
To feel you move
Within the safety
Of my womb.

To feel the pain and joy
Of giving birth:
A mix of emotions present
Throughout parenthood.

How I have dreamed
Of holding you close,
Feeling you suckle
At my breast.

Smelling the scent
Peculiar to you,
And hearing your cry
For attention and love.

How I have imagined
Your growing,
Who you might look like,
Your going to school.

Wondering what your
Interests might be:
Music, nature, sports,
History, law, writing?

But, my child,
My dreams are mere fantasy,
None of this will happen,
I am empty.

The love I have stored
Has turned to grief
As I realise for sure
You will never be.

I Longed To Hold You

I longed to hold you in my arms,
I longed to watch you grow,
Hear you laugh, watch you play,
To teach you and learn from you.

I longed to be there in your need,
I longed to hear you call for me,
To sooth your fears, wipe your tears,
To share until peace and joy return.

But it is not to be, my little one,
I am not to hold you in my arms,
For God longed to hold you too,
To watch you grow, hear you laugh…

God's desire for you must be great, my child,
For he called you back to himself
Before life had hardly begun,
And I am left with a space in my heart,
That you will never fill.

Good News?

"You heard my news" she said,
As something squeezed my heart
Making breathing difficult,
My eyes filled with tears.

Then a stranger's voice,
Not mine,
"Yes, we heard,"
It came again as panic rose,
"Yes, we heard."

I felt claustrophobic,
Just needed to get out,
Trapped.
Wanted to cry out
When he said,
"When is it due?"

Everything in me screamed,
But all I heard was that small voice,
"Yes, we heard"
Then a forced smile,
As my heart ached with pain
Because your pregnancy
Wasn't mine.

New Birth

'I am barren,' I said,
And yes, I will never feel
My baby move within,
Or know the pains of childbirth,
Or feel the suckling
Of my little one at my breast.

But I know another birthing,
Another bringing to birth.

I helped you find within
Confidence to lead others in prayer,
And you I helped to preach.
Another to find his way when lost,
And other still to find light in their darkness.

I cannot birth my own child,
And that pains me
More than I can say,
But new birth is happening all around,
And I am a part of it.

Sunrise: Resurrection

The tears of darkness are dried
By the Sun's power;
Sorrow is no more,
And joy fills the air.

The Path to God

I stand in my own path
Blocking the way.
I am eager to go forward,
Yet blocking the way.

I cannot see what's ahead
And blocking the way
Determined but fear wins,
As I block the way.

I see a light ahead,
Still blocking the way,
Quietly I speak,
I turn and understand.

The way now clear,
I walk past myself.
'Til fear grips again
And I block the way.

God's Fingerprints

"O Lord, our Lord, How Majestic is your name in all the earth"
(Psalm 8:1)

I am surrounded by Your
Holy name, Lord.

The trees announce your glory,
The flowers proclaim Your splendour,
The sea tells of Your power and gentleness.

The mountains shout of Your strength,
The sky reminds of Your protective wing,
The birds sing of Your faithfulness.

The whole of nature proclaims
Your Holy Name,
Your fingerprints are
Seen on all I see.

Lily

Kissed by the sun you
Turn and open your face.
I see into your mysterious being
And your beauty draws me deeper.

Soaking up the sun's rays you
Become more and more open,
Gently moving your body to
Follow its walk across the sky.

Silently, without a word,
You call me closer;
Hypnotised by your radiance
I gladly respond.

My breath is taken as I see
"The drink of the gods"
Flowing freely along your stamen.
You invite me to drink.

Such sweet nectar!
What a priceless gift
Given from one so regal
To one as humble as me!

What Wonder It Is Lord.

What wonder it is, Lord,
That in the midst of the awesome beauty
Of all your creation,
You love and care for me.

Praise the Lord!

You trees, raise your arms high and
Praise the Lord!
You meadow flowers turn your faces and
Praise the Lord!
You mountains, lift your voices and
Praise the Lord!
You seas, call out His name and
Praise the Lord!
You birds, sing out a joyful song and
Praise the Lord!
You herds and flocks, you gorse and grasses,
You rivers and springs, you insects and spiders,
Let us all,
Praise the Lord!

The Creator and Creation

The created turned their
Backs on the Creator God:
Death's strong hold gripped
Their lives like a vice.

God's call to return was
Heard but again forgotten;
The Creator's heart bled at
The sight of His ruined creation.

The Creator spoke
In order to save His people;
His Word was born
In Jesus, child of God.

Sunday Church

It's Sunday and
The Folk are gathering
At church again.
Each one has a
Story to tell.
Each has things on
Their mind.

She's upset, having
Argued with her husband.
The woman over there would
Rather be somewhere else,
While that birthday child there is
Bursting with excitement.

The irritated man has forced
His children along, and they
Drag their feet, dreaming
Of computer games, T.V. and football.

The lady at the back
Is suffering arthritic pain,
And the man in blue
Cries inside where no-one knows.
Some joyfully clap their hands,
Others silently scream.

So many people, so many stories,
So much pain, so much joy,
All coming together to worship
The God who,
No matter how they feel,
Loves them more than they
Can ever know.

God's Family

You are my sister,
Yet you know nothing of me.
You are my brother,
Yet you don't know my name.

You are my mother,
Yet you have not borne me.
My family surround me,
Yet I am alone.

Is this how our Father
Wanted it to be?
Together, but alien,
In our own safe boxes?

With the odd smile, and "hello",
Eyes that say,
"Don't come near",
Is that how we are to be?

How can I love, and
Allow others to love me?
How can I trust
This, God's family?

God's Word Of Love

God's Word of Love was
Revealed in the birth of Jesus.
God Himself came to
Show the way back to Him.

This child brings us
From darkness to light,
From death to life,
From separation to friendship.

The one we have waited for
Is now with us.
Take His hand of Love,
And come to Him.

A Candle Flame

A single flame
In a darkened room,
Bringing warmth,
Hope and light.

Dancing in
The moving air,
Then, pausing, still,
Before proceeding.

How you calm
My frantic fears;
How you bring peace
Into my chaos.

A candle flame
In a darkened room,
Symbol of The Light
Enveloping my life.

A Tree of Life

You feed me,
Causing me to grow,
To unfurl myself –
To reach out and up,
Like a new shoot
Making its way out of the soil
Into the day-light,
Reaching out towards the sun,

You feed me:
Rain, light,
You are with me,
Even in the dark, cold
Earth of my being.
You are in my tightly curled up leaves.
In there.
Feeding, coaxing, encouraging, enabling;
Dancing in my new growth,
Staying with me
Until I am ready to unfurl some more,
Staying with me always,
Growing me into
A Tree of Life.

The Sacrament

Invited to choose
A piece of fruit
To meditate on
I chose you.

My eyes feasted
Upon your flesh,
Speckled with yellow seed
And topped with crown of green.

My fingers felt
Your unusual texture,
Outlined your heart shape,
And identified your creases.

Invited to smell
Your fragrance,
Your sweetness filled my senses,
And my mouth watered.

Then I was asked to
Cut you in two,
I took the knife
And cut from top to bottom.

Your juice ran red
On both knife and serviette,
My breath was taken and
I wanted to fall to my knees.

But I remained in my seat,
As the image of
My Lord's body on and taken from
The cross unfolded.

"Now cut your fruit
Into smaller pieces,
And share it with
Those around you"

I hardly dare take
Up the invitation,
Yet, with an effort,
I took the knife and cut.

As I cut your flesh
I became aware of
My sin, my part
In the cross.

And as I shared
Your flesh with others,
I heard the words,
"This is my body, broken for you."

The Cross

I am afraid, Lord,
Even though I know
In truth you are here,
I am fearful of what is to come.

Remember my words,
"Take this cup away",
And know I understand
The fear you feel.

People say, Lord, "Have faith",
"God's with you, "Be at peace,"
And I feel guilt
As anxiety overwhelms.

Remember my sweat,
Like droplets of blood,
And know that anxiety
Doesn't have to mean 'no faith'.

I shy away, Lord,
From the company of others
Rather than seeking
Prayer and fellowship.

Remember that I too
Chose to be alone,
And be who you are,
Not what's expected.

I fear, Lord, that I might
Lose you amidst all
The pain and grief,
Felt now, and to come.

Remember my words,
"Father, why forsake me?"
And know I am with you
In your dark emptiness.

It's been going on
So long, Lord, the pain,
Physical, mental, emotional,
I fear there will be no end.

Remember the nails,
The long, slow death,
And know I know
Your prolonged agony.

But remember too, child,
My resurrection, and know,
As you share my cross,
You will also share my Life.

The Beginning

This is not an ending, but a beginning,
We have been on a journey,
Now we've arrived at the end,
But it is here where everything else starts.

This is not 'goodbye', but 'see you later',
The old pattern of things will cease,
But we, both individually and corporately,
Walk in the same direction to our God.

Tears may be shed, and grief felt,
But joy too will flood in.
Our paths will now separate,
But a part of you will go with me.

We are different and separate,
Yet one,
A part of each living in the other,
And God holds us all in his hand.

The Potter

You hold me in your hands,
Just as a potter holds the clay.
With skill and gentleness
You tirelessly work with me,
Watering my dry places,
Making me supple,
Your hands working constantly:
Breaking, moulding, smoothing, shaping,
Expertly guiding me
Into the being you'd have me be,
And with each touch you leave
An impression of your fingertips,
Which become a part of me.

Reach Out Your Hand, Lord

Our world is hurting, Lord;
There's so much loneliness and fear.
Hear our cry for help,
Have mercy, grant peace, bring love.

Reach out your hand, Lord,
To our hurting world;
Quell the fears, teach us to care,
Help us reach out to each other as one.

A teenage girl in despair
Silently commits suicide,
Another old man dies
In loneliness and fear.

Reach out your hand, Lord,
To our hurting world;
Quell the fears, teach us to care,
Help us reach out to each other as one.

Neglected by hurting parents,
A child cries in hunger.
Seeking to numb their pain,
Young people turn to drugs and drink.

Reach out your hand, Lord,
To our hurting world;
Quell the fears, teach us to care,
Help us reach out to each other as one.

Brought low by unemployment,
A man stares into nothingness.
A woman begs on the streets,
Having no home, no food, no one to love.

Reach out your hand, Lord,
To our hurting world;
Quell the fears, teach us to care,
Help us reach out to each other as one.

The old woman locks her door,
Fearful of the world outside,
Whilst many others find home
The most unsafe place to be.

Reach out your hand, Lord,
To our hurting world;
Quell the fears, teach us to care,
Help us reach out to each other as one.

Nation makes war against nation,
People are forced to leave their homes,
A child is bullied in the playground,
Simply for wearing the 'wrong' shoes.

Reach out your hand, Lord,
To our hurting world;
Quell the fears, teach us to care,
Help us reach out to each other as one.

Lives full of hopelessness,
Broken relationships, broken people,
Come now, reach out your hand,
Heal us, heal your world, O Lord.

Reach out your hand, Lord,
To our hurting world;
Quell the fears, teach us to care,
Help us reach out to each other as one.

You Reached Out

You reached out
To the hurting,
The lonely, and the outcast,
You ask me to do the same,
And to start with me.

You showed how
To befriend an enemy,
To forgive and to love,
You ask me to do the same,
And to start with me.

You embraced
The whole person,
The good and the bad,
You ask me to do the same,
And to start with me.

It's hard, Lord, to accept, befriend,
Forgive, embrace and love myself,
But you ask me to greet everyone
As if I were greeting you,
And to start with me.

Be Still

I struggle against
The waves of life,
I gasp for breath in
The cold, dark waters.

My arms and legs
Work in panic,
But I move no closer
To the shore.

"Be still", you call,
But I continue fighting,
Fearful of the freezing waters,
And the death that might follow.

"Be still", you say,
"Relax, be still."
"But I can't", I think,
"I'm going to drown, to freeze."

"Be still", you repeat
In urgency,
"Then it will be
Easier to pull you in"

At last I understand
And put all my effort,
And all my strength
Into being still.

I rest on the safety belt
Around my waist,
Waiting to be pulled ashore,
But the fears rise again.

My Arms and legs panic
Into frenzied action again,
And you call out,
"Be Still."

Snowdon

Your majesty and splendour
Are veiled in cloud;
I strain my eyes
To see your glory,
But it is all in vain.

Then the cloud lifts,
Rising, it reveals your beauty,
I am awed as I glimpse
A mere fraction of the fullness
Of Your being.

God Dawns On Me

You reach out
And show God's care to me,
You teach and guide
And show God's concern to me,
You laugh
And show God's delight to me,
You shed tears
And show God's heart to me,
You restore and heal,
And show God's compassion to me,
You grieve,
And show God's sorrow to me,
You accept
And show God's mercy to me,
You die on a cross
And show God's love to me.

Awaken my senses

Awaken my senses, Lord,
That I might see you in
The opening leaf buds of trees,
The smile of a stranger,
The work of an artist.

Awaken my senses, Lord,
That I might hear you
In scripture, poetry and song,
In the crashing of waves,
In tears and laugher.

Awaken my senses, Lord,
That I might smell you
In the fragrance of a rose,
In linen, fresh from the washing line,
In the sweat of work and toil.

Awaken my senses, Lord,
That I might taste you,
In the flesh of an orange,
In raindrops on my tongue,
In a refreshing cup of tea.

Awaken my senses, Lord,
That I might feel you,
In the intimacy of a lover,
In pebble, shell and wood,
In the chair, in which I sit and rest.

Awaken my senses, Lord,
That I might know you.

Freedom And Life

You cowered against a wall
Like a frightened animal.
Part of me wanted to reach out,
To bring you into freedom and life,
But a greater part of me wanted
To push you into darkness and death.

You looked neglected, dirty,
Rejected by all, unloved,
I felt I should reach out
To show compassion, acceptance and love,
But a greater part of me wanted
To push you away, to reject you again.

I looked at you with
Anger and with fear,
Anger that you are
No better than life has made you,
And fear that you may
Be found out, found to be here.

But as I look again,
I look with compassion,
I find I want to reach out,
But fear makes this simple act difficult.

As I look closer,
I see a child, a fearful child,
I look and see myself and realise
That loving you, I love myself,
Accepting you, I accept myself,
Reaching out, giving you freedom and life,
I free myself and live.

God's Beauty

The hills, rocks and fields
Are kissed by the sun's rays,
Leaves of the trees turn to gold,
There is the blue of kingfisher,
Red of the goldfinch, the yellowhammer;
Songs from blackbird, robin and wren,
Creation's beauty sings
An anthem of harmony,
Forming a rainbow
Of colour and sound
But your beauty, O God,
Is a beauty even greater than this,
Infinitely more beautiful,
Without beginning, or end.

My Spirit Dances

My spirit dances
In your presence, O Lord,
My soul soars and flies,
Delighting in you.

Taking my hand
You cause me to spin,
My whole being rejoices
With your touch.

You dance with me,
And laugh with me,
As my soul reaches
New heights in you.

The Stone

Cold to touch, yet warmed when held,
Hard, but not impenetrable,
Some have made avenues
Into my inner being:
Windows bringing light to my centre;
Others have taken refuge
And have become a part of me.
Moulded and shaped by outside forces,
I remain what, who I am.

Love, Flood My Being

Love, extravagant and intimate,
Love, patient and kind,
Love, gentle and merciful,
Flood my being with Yourself.

Love, mysterious, yet known,
Love, overwhelming, yet desired,
Love, Almighty, yet friend,
Flood my being with Yourself.

Love, holy and true,
Hold me in your arms,
Cause me to dance to Your song,
As you flood my being with Yourself.

Labels

Labels weigh heavily:
Images others have of me,
Often out of focus with my own,
Their expectations, impressions,
Formed over a moment, a minute,
Or, for some, several years,
But All Distorted:
All more or less than I am.

Labels weigh heavily,
Burdens I attach to myself,
No less Distorted.
I find, I find wholeness, my True Self
In God alone:
I am who I am in Him.

The thought scares me, yet,
My being yearns for Him,
To be who I am,
To fly, to be free:
De-labelled.

Grief

I feel sore in my soul
My heart aches,
I feel my soul is bruised,
My inner being clenched with grief,
My body is pulled down,
My body is fatigued beyond measure;
My mind is muddled and numb,
There is no clarity in my thinking.
My loss is great,
Loss disables,
Steals me from myself,
Grief envelops me,
Inner sobs and torment
Manifest in silent weeping.

Listen

(Ps 85:8 – 'I am listening. What is God's message?)

Listen with your eyes,
See the broken shell,
Half missing, dirty, cracked.

Listen with your touch,
Hold it gently in your hand,
Smooth, fragile, incomplete.

Listen with your imagination;
See the new life emerging,
Crying for food, warmth and comfort.

Listen with your ears,
Hear the bird's melodic song,
Bright, light, rejoicing.

Listen with all your senses
To the message I give you
Let your heart dance,
Let your soul fly, for
From your brokenness and fragility,
New life emerges, singing.

The Spirit's Gifts: Your Gift is Mine

Falling like autumn leaves,
God's Spirit pours out her gifts,
Different colours,
Different shapes,
Each for the good of all,
And all for each.

Delighting and eager to share,
She scatters her gifts abundantly,
Gifting you,
Gifting me,
Willing each to grow,
To live, to dance and be free.

But I sadden the Spirit's heart,
When I see your giftedness, for,
I am envious,
And I grieve
For what I cannot do,
And am blind to what I can.

'Don't you understand?' She asks,
'That I gift them for you, so
You may dance,
You may live?
I gift them for you,
And for them, I gift you.'

I initially wrote 'Love Me' with my name, where is says, 'child'.
I'd been thinking about when Jesus asked Peter if he loved him. Using
the imagination I entered the scene and heard Jesus asking me the
question, 'Do you love me' and I kept saying that I did – this stayed
with me all day, 'Do you love me?' 'Yes' then silence. Thinking about
Jesus' response to Peter, after he'd asked him the question, I asked the
Lord why he didn't give me a task as he had Peter, "Because I want you
to see that loving me is enough" came the reply.

Love me

'Child, do you love me?'
'I do love you, Lord,
like the daisy which,
touched by the sun,
opens in worship and joy.'

'Child, do you love me?'
'I do love you, Lord,
like the chaffinch, who
throws back his head and
sings with the thrill of being alive.'

'Child, do you love me?'
'I do love you, Lord,
like the eagle that soars
the mountains and valleys
marvelling your wondrous creation.'

'Child, do you love me?'
'I do love you, Lord,
like the burning sun,
painting the earth in a myriad of colour
as it rises.'

'Child, do you love me?'
'I do love you, Lord,
You are my heartbeat, my very breath,
In you I find my meaning,
I do love you.'

'Yes, I know you love me,
And that is all I ask of you:
to be who you are,
true to me and to yourself,
and love me.'

Nature's Hug

Feeling down-hearted and sad,
Longing for human touch:
A healing, loving hug,
I walked in the meadow.

I watched the merry dance
Of bees, searching nectar,
Smelt the sweet fragrance
That comes after rain.

I startled a hidden grouse,
Who flew and startled me;
I smiled at lupin rainwater,
Caught to give someone a drink.

I sat for a while on a bench,
Watching a wren who scolded
Sharply and persistently my presence,
'I won't hurt you little wren,' I said.

Then a woodpecker called out,
From the top of the tallest tree.
Spirits lifted, I wandered back,
Realising I'd had nature's hug.

I wrote *Demons* after praying with Mark 5:1-20,
using imaginative meditation.

Demons

Hidden demons taunt,
As young as when first met,
Crippling now, as then,
Trapping me in their net.

Vicious laughter sounds,
Calls of, 'Not good enough!'
'Mistake, you were, mistake,
And you want to be loved?'

The demons crowd me in,
Marring all I do,
Crippling me with fear, til,
I want to be someone new.

'Name them,' Jesus says,
'Name them; give them to me.
I'll throw them in the abyss,
And this yourself will see.'

So in tears I name them all,
Feeling each one anew,
I give them over to Jesus,
Trusting what he said he'll do.

I wrote the following after meditating on
Ephesians 1 & 3:14-21

I am the Daughter of the King

I am the daughter of the King,
He loves me with an immeasurable love:
High and deep and broad.

I am the daughter of the King,
He placed his kiss, his seal on my head,
I am his chosen one.

I am the daughter of the King,
He gives me riches beyond price:
Wisdom, knowledge, hope and peace.

I am the daughter of the King,
His rich heritage is there for me,
His power and rule keep me safe.

I am the daughter of the King,
He dances with me, he laughs with me,
He holds me in his hand and heart.

I am the daughter of the King.

A New Name

I give you a new name,
O child of mine,
A name of freedom,
Of peace and safety.

I give you a name
That has always been yours,
But your heart, too sad,
Could not hear or receive.

I give you a new name,
Of courage and hope,
Of life and of love,
Of joy and rejoicing.

'Daughter' you'll be,
I'm your Heavenly Father,
The father of your dreams and more,
From now and for all eternity.

The following was written after meditating on a photograph of an iris, on which rested a bee.

The Iris and the Bee

The flowering glory of the iris:
Purple-blue petals
Patterned richly with gold, white and red
Belie spring growing pains
And winter's struggle.

The delicately painted petals'
Beautifully etched intricate veins
Reach every part, enhancing, feeding,
Belying their ever rooted connection
To the messiness of where her life began.

She opens her heart to another,
Offering rest and sustenance
From her rich bounty.
Belying her hesitant emerging from
Dark hiding into vulnerability and strength.

The unfurling, unfolding beauty,
Revealing her very self,
Receiving, sharing, giving,
Speaks of God's invitation
To struggle, to grow, to flower.

The following was written after meditating
with a spruce cone.

The Spruce Cone

Circular growing,
Yet never returning
To exactly the same place,
Each circuit bringing new growth,
A different perspective,
An upward, unending spiral
Of delicate strength,
Responding from within
And to external forces:
Now opening, now closing tight,
Now protecting precious seed,
Now dispersing seed with abandon,
Now singing with the wind,
Now in silent stillness,
All this and more:
The simple complexity of who I am.

Nature Rests

Gold and crimson whispers
Across painted sky
Surround dark cloud mountains.

Blackbirds sing their goodnights,
Woodland chatter quietens to a hush...
Then silence, as nature rests.

Yet, under dark blanket
Her heart beats with joy and hope:
Life is not lost;

The bat awakens,
Silently dancing on the wing,
Mindful of his sleeping neighbours.

The owl hoots a sweet lullaby
Which enters the dreams of those who sleep,
Ensuing rest, with assurance of a new tomorrow.

Sunset

Blood red streaks
Stretch across the sky,
Piercing the darkness
Of black cloud.

Redeeming scarlet
Gives hope of new dawn
As a dark shroud covers all,
Announcing day's end.

'Submit to the Lord'
(James 4)

The Lord holds me
In the palm of his hand,
He feels my hesitation,
My reluctance and desire.

The Lord holds me,
In patience and with love,
Breaking down my barriers,
Removing, with care, my masks.

The Lord holds me,
His warmth is seeping through,
Slowly melting my cold heart,
Causing me to live anew.

The Lord holds me,
Singing gentle love songs,
Softly calling out my name,
Inviting me closer in.

The Lord holds me,
I listen to his voice,
I listen to his presence,
I listen to his silence.

The Lord holds me,
Moulds me and changes me,
Takes me deep into his heart,
Until I am his own.

Monologues & Meditations

The use of Monologues and Meditations

Monologues and meditations can be used within worship services, small groups and in personal prayer. Before each, ensure that those taking part are relaxed and focused, putting distractions to one side, if possible; pray for the guidance of the Holy Spirit.

The monologues written here are imagined voices of characters in the Bible. They can be read dramatically, as a part of corporate worship, in order to give a different dimension to the Bible reading of the day or they can be used in small groups.

In a small group, the leader may or may not choose to start by reading the Bible text where the character of the monologue is based. The monologue should be read dramatically before inviting the group to comment on what struck them about it, how they felt and what they thought; comments can then be used as a springboard to discussion.

Monologues can be used in a similar way within personal prayer. Read the monologue through a couple of times, listening to your feelings as well as the words on the page – notice what you react to and what that reaction is: resistance, joy, hope, doubt… Then put the monologue aside and talk to God about your experience. You may like to write your reflections in a journal.

There are no hard and fast rules – use the monologues in the way(s) that you find most helpful.

The imaginative meditation is, not surprisingly, using the imagination in prayer or meditation. Ordinarily, it is used by taking a Bible passage and imagining being there, watching the scene unfolding before you as if you were there, taking in the sounds, sights, textures, aromas and tastes. You may choose to be a bystander or one of the characters in the text.

Most of the meditations in this book take that form, of taking a character and imagining being the character in a Bible passage but two are different, one is a meditation on a sunflower seed and one is entitled, 'Try and Try again'. The latter was written as part of a prayer course that I was co-leading; the subject of the session was about perseverance and keeping going in prayer.

The meditations here have been written in such a way as to be used to lead a group but they can be used in private prayer or corporate worship. Again, there are no hard and fast rules. Here are some simple guidelines:

- Ensure before starting that those taking part take time to relax, invite the Holy Spirit to guide you in your prayer.

- Give those taking part permission to stay with any point of the meditation that they feel led to stay with.

- Inform the group that there will be a period of silence after the meditation.

- Give appropriate pauses throughout the reading of the meditation, in order to give time for the scene to unfold and for those taking part to experience what is happening to them within the meditation. Don't be tempted to rush on; be gentle.

- At the end of the meditation, leave a good time of silence – the amount of time depends on the experience of the group and the time constraints of the service/meeting. For a group who are not used to silences, it may be that three to four minutes is enough, for a group used to silence, an hour or more might be used. Think about how to bring the silence to an end – if it has been a long silence and people have moved from the meeting place, it may be that you play a piece of music as a signal to come back, it may be that you give a time or it may be, if the group have stayed together, that you give a warning that the end of the silence is imminent thirty seconds or so before the end.

- Invite people to share their experiences of the time of prayer. Ensure that people feel free to only share what they choose to and not to share if they do not want to.

- Listen to what is shared and thank those who share.

- End with a moment's silence and a prayer.

Using the imagination in prayer comes easier to some people than others. Some find it easier to be led in such prayer; some find it hard to get going but when they do, stay with it for a long time; others find it easy to get into it but hard to stay with it; for some, it leaves them cold and isn't helpful at all. It is good to remember that we are all different and that there are many different ways of praying, imaginative meditation is just one such way; what you find helpful in prayer, another may not, it doesn't mean that your way of praying is wrong or that theirs is – it is just different; a different way of being with God. However, it can be good, from time to time, to try something different or something we have tried before and that did not previously sit comfortably with us: in doing so, we may find ourselves surprised and blessed.

Please use these meditations in the way(s) you find most helpful.

Monologue: John the Baptist

As I was growing up, my parents (and our neighbours) used to tell me what happened when I was born; how Father wasn't able to speak all the time Mother was pregnant, right up until I was named. Father would say that my name, John, was given to me by God. To be honest, I didn't take that much notice at first but as I grew, I began to wonder what it meant; something stirred in me. Father used to sing a song about me, saying that I would be a prophet, that I would prepare the way for the Lord. 'Me! How can I prepare the way?' I thought.

I was a good student and, given what my father had told me, I particularly searched the great books of the prophets. There, the coming of the Lord is described like waters flowing and flowers blossoming in the desert. I've seen that happen in the desert, after the rains come: you wouldn't believe the transformation; it was hard to believe that it was the same parched place it had been. Could it be that the coming of the Lord meant such a transformation in the lives of his people too? It seemed so, for I learnt that the coming of the Lord meant that the deaf would hear, those who couldn't walk would, those who were imprisoned would be freed and those who couldn't speak would sing for joy. How I longed for that day; others did too but so many had forgotten God's promise or didn't understand what it meant or had given up on the idea he would come.

'You will prepare the way for the Lord,' Father used to say. The prophet Isaiah spoke of one preparing the way for the Lord, telling people to make straight paths, to raise the valleys, to bring down the mountains and hills, to clear away the rocks and stones, enabling God's glory to be revealed. 'But what does it mean?' I used to say, 'Surely I'm not to literally bring down the mountains and fill-in the valleys – how could that be? Who could do such a thing?' I kept searching the scriptures and found the prophets repeatedly talking about justice for the poor, caring for the needy and I thought hard about these things but it wasn't until I went into the desert and started to teach that I really fully grasped what it meant.

Sometimes I would get so frustrated, so angry, when people thought they would be saved by God simply because of their descent from Abraham or they thought they could come and be baptised, then get on with their lives as before but baptism was a symbol of change, not the cure or a talisman, enabling the sinner to continue to sin and a promise of redemption anyway; the fruitfulness of their lives was like rotting figs that had long ago fallen from the tree. I'd say, 'Produce fruit in keeping with repentance; if you have two tunics, give one to someone who has none.' Then they started shouting out, asking what they were to do. Tax collectors I told not to collect more than they were due; soldiers I told not to extort money or give false witness, to be content with their pay.'

As I spoke I was reminded of the mountains and the valleys, the crooked roads and the boulders that needed clearing and I realised that greed, selfishness, injustice, and all those things that trap us as human beings, were the mountains that needed to be brought down, these were the valleys that needed filling in, the roads that needed straightening, and the rocks and stones that needed to be cleared, to make the highway of God ready for his coming.

I only saw the 'mountains' and the 'valleys', the big things that were obviously in the way of God's coming; I know that there would have been more subtle things: the rocks and stones, hidden away in the hearts of men and women, that only they and God knew about; moving the bigger things would bring the smaller things to light. Then, with God's help, they could be moved too. I saw it happen, lives were changed, continue to be changed.

I wonder what I would see as the mountains and valleys in your lives; where are the winding roads and the rocks and boulders that get in the way, that get between you and God? Are there situations that are taking you away from God or maybe certain people do that? Or is it something in you? Your attitudes, behaviour, fears...? Whatever it is, are you willing to make that change, to prepare the highway to your heart for God? Would you be one of the ones who listened to me and choose to be baptised or would you be one of the many who mocked, then walked away, taking their mountains and valleys, winding roads and rocks with them?

The Lord is coming, are you prepared?

Monologue: Mary

It is almost time now for the birth of my son. Yes, I know my baby is a boy, it's a long story, some say it's a 'tall story' but it *is* true. I'll tell you about it.

I was minding my own business, humming a little tune, as I washed the plates after our midday meal, almost nine months ago now, when there was suddenly a man in the room with me: gave me a shock, I can tell you!

He said to me, 'Greetings, favoured one of God, the Lord is with you.' I didn't need a stranger to tell me the Lord was with me, I just wanted him to get out of my parents' house, 'What will people say? What will *Joseph* and my parents say?' I kept thinking. I was so worried.

'Don't be afraid Mary', the stranger said. What did he think I was going to be – a strange man in my parent's house, me here alone – how did he get in and how on earth did he know my name? All this was going through my mind and it was as if he could read my thoughts. 'Don't be afraid' he said. Well, if I wasn't afraid then, which I was, what he said next would make sure I would be!

'You are going to conceive and have a son,' he said.

'How can you know that, me and Joseph aren't even married yet, let alone...'

'Joseph won't be the father', he said, I backed away. 'I'm a virgin and it's going to stay that way until me and Joseph are married,' I said.

'Don't be afraid, Mary,' I would have laughed if I hadn't been so afraid! Don't be afraid? How did he want me to feel?

'The Lord is pleased with you; very pleased,' he said.

'What are you talking about?' I said.

'You will conceive and give birth to a son, God's Holy Spirit will cause this to happen and the child will be called the Son of God; you will call him Jesus.'

I stared at him, astonished but that funny feeling I often get inside, when I know that God is speaking to me, started to stir and I listened more closely.

'Your relative Elizabeth is six months pregnant and people said that she would never have a child; God made it happen for her.'

'Yes', I thought, 'I'd heard about that; Zechariah had been struck dumb when an angel called Gabriel came to him and told him he'd have a son – he could only communicate through writing until John was born.

'I am Gabriel', the stranger said. I thought about what he had said to me about the baby, I questioned him he answered my questions then he waited in silence as I thought about what he had said.

The Lord had chosen me to have a child. His child. How would I explain that to my parents, let alone Joseph? Would they believe me? Would this child be the saviour we have been waiting for? It's what the name Jesus means but it's a popular name... Then there was Zechariah and Elizabeth: who could deny what had happened to them? And then there was that deep feeling inside that said, 'it *is* God who is speaking.'

I don't know how long he waited but he didn't rush me. I began to realise that although I could say, 'No' I wanted to say 'Yes' because this was God asking something of me and he had given so much to me, so very much. I knew that it wasn't going to be easy but God would be with me – in me even!

'Okay, yes, let it be as you say' I said. He smiled and was gone.

I felt so alone yet excited too. Did I dream it? I knew that the one person who would understand was Elizabeth. Gabriel had reminded me of Elizabeth; I knew I needed to talk to her, to be with her to share with her what had happened. So I went and, oh, what joy we shared! I stayed three months, right up to John's birth – what joy when his father wrote the baby's name then sang in praise of God and the son he had given. I laid my hand on my belly, knowing that I too had a special child inside me: a god-child.

Facing Joseph wasn't quite so easy. I thought he'd be furious but he wasn't; he was deeply hurt. The pain was written on his face, I think it would have been easier if he had shouted and got angry but he didn't. He said that he wouldn't make public what I'd 'done' – I kept telling him that I hadn't 'done' anything, just said 'Yes' to God but he didn't believe me. I cried and he cried too. I wondered what God was playing at, bringing me to this...

God forgive me, I shouldn't have doubted. Joseph came to see me a few days later, telling me that *he* was sorry; he said that he still didn't understand but that God had spoken to him in a dream and had explained that the child was God's own and I was true to Joseph. It still wasn't easy for either of us, there were snide comments, sniggers in the streets and frowns and shaking of heads everywhere we went. When we discovered we had to journey to Bethlehem because of the census, although I knew it wouldn't be easy, it was a kind of relief: at least we'd get away from the gossips and pointed stares.

It was a nightmare when we got to Bethlehem; I'd been dreaming of being able to sit down and put my feet up: 80 miles we'd walked. When we got here though, we couldn't find anywhere to stay; place is packed. Joseph was going spare, then a kindly Inn Keeper, seeing my condition, offered us some space in his stable – as long as I could sit down, I didn't care anymore, though after the first ten minutes I started to fret about my boy. How will I give birth in this place? I know the time is near now.

Then I felt that deep down feeling again – We are where God wants us to be, it'll be okay, he'll show us the way.

There is something that has crossed my mind many times these past few months: 'why me?' I've often wondered, 'What is it that God saw in me, to choose me as the one to carry his son and give birth to him?'

My friend, Martha, said that it was because He knew I'd say, 'Yes.' I don't know, I may have said 'yes' but not before I'd asked lots of questions first. Ester said it was because I'd be a good mother and that I'm caring, patient and compassionate but I also know that I can be the opposite of those things too. I think myself that it is because I believed – I had faith and trusted what he said would be would be; yes, I questioned but I don't think God minds that, it helps to find out what he wants us to do. I know that whatever he saw in me he gave me in the first place and the only thing I could do was to offer that back and in saying, 'yes' that's what I was doing.

I wonder, have you ever thought about what God sees when he looks at you? Have you thought about what he sees and how he wants you to use what he has given you?

A Monologue: A Woman Suffering from Bleeding
(Mark 5:24b-34 / Luke 8:42b-48)

Some have asked me how I managed to do it; if they'd think about it just for a few seconds, they would realise that I simply had no other choice: all my options had been used up some time before.

Yes, I was scared, so scared I felt sick with fear but I was also desperate. I had been bleeding for twelve years. Do you know how draining that is, how humiliating and isolating? I was an outcast. The woman's lot is to endure a few days of monthly bleeding, it is the natural way of things; during that time woman are unclean but after the ritual bath they are accepted again into the heart of the family and what a wonderful feeling that is for her. It happened that one month, my bleeding started unexpectedly and it just wouldn't stop. Oh yes, I'd seen doctors, many doctors, only it got to a point where I couldn't afford to. I had spent all I had on doctors but rather than getting better, I got worse.

So, I wrapped a scarf around my head and covered my face, so as not to be recognised. Many women wear scarves, so I didn't look out of place and I just joined the crowd. I had heard stories about Jesus and I had heard him speak, listening to him I knew that he was someone special. I knew that I couldn't go up to him but I thought that if I could just touch his cloak as he walked by, I would be healed, I was sure of it.

I was making my way through the crowd who were stood around Jesus, listening to him, when I saw someone approach him. Jesus then started to walk away with the man, my heart sank but the crowd moved too and I was swept along with them. I knew I had nothing to lose so I moved as quickly as I could through the crowd, towards him. I pushed myself forward, which wasn't easy, as the bleeding had always brought with it pain and discomfort, made worse with walking and movement, so the jostling of the crowd aggravated it and I kept my mouth closed and cried inwardly, in pain, so as to not draw attention to myself. I was fearful as to what they might do to me, if they knew who I was and what was wrong with me.

Everyone was pushing and shoving, it turned out that that was a good thing for me because it meant that Jesus wasn't moving fast to get to wherever he was going to and I was able to get close enough to reach out. I knew I was close enough; I just had to reach out my hand. I took a deep breath, looked for my escape route, then looked back to where Jesus was and reached out.

It was over.

I knew it was over immediately I touched Jesus' cloak; I knew because the pain had gone and I knew that with it, the bleeding had stopped too. I felt free, released from the prison I had been in for twelve long years. It all happened in a matter of moments – I reached out, I touched, I knew I was healed and I turned and started to walk away. The crowd stopped moving and I felt that fear again, as I heard Jesus' voice ask, 'Who touched me?' I closed my eyes and cried silently within, 'Oh no!' I started walking away again as I heard his followers laugh and say that many people were touching him, it was the crowd. But he knew, he knew something had happened and I knew that I wasn't going to get away, I had tried but had been caught. I turned, lowered my scarf, at which a number of people cried out who I was and those around me stepped back, so as not to be contaminated, my heart ached. I walked back towards Jesus, I began to cry, I fell at Jesus feet and told him everything, how I'd been ill for so long, had nothing left, how I had just known that if I could just touch his cloak, I would be healed, that's all I'd asked, to touch his cloak and in touching, I knew I'd be made well.

So I touched and I was right: I was well. I bowed my head, waiting for his reproach.

But he didn't reproach me. He crouched down to where I was on the floor and touched my shoulder and I looked up and he smiled – he touched me, it was the first touch of love I had felt for years. It was like the crowd wasn't there anymore, it was just him and me, he looked into my eyes with such intensity and such love, it was like he was trying to read my very soul, then he spoke, 'Daughter, your faith has healed you,' he said, 'go in peace.' I closed my eyes again and I breathed, it was as if I had been holding my breath for an age then I cried, I cried because of the tenderness of his words and his touch, I cried for the years I had lost and the friends I had lost and my family and I cried for joy for I was free.

Monologue: Martha
(Luke 10:38-42)

I remember the day so clearly. I invited Jesus to stay. Of course, I knew that it wouldn't be just Jesus... People kept arriving and asking, "Is Jesus here?" And I ushered them in whilst inviting them to stay for a meal.

Things went quite well at first; I felt good and happy. It was always good to see Jesus, and I wanted everything to be just right... "Mary will come and help soon", I thought... There was a knock at the door and another friend entered. "Come in," I said cheerily, "go through, and do stay for something to eat... Ask Mary to come help will you...?" They went into the other room, but Mary didn't come... I thought that she must be pouring drinks for our guests or something...

The day was hot, and I was getting hot too... Then it seemed that things began to start going wrong; I'm not sure what set the ball rolling, but I just kept thinking how I had wanted everything to be so right, which seemed to make things go even more wrong...

Knocking that cup of flour over was the last straw... I decided to go and get Mary myself. I took some fresh drinks with me... I was astonished when I got in there; she wasn't pouring drinks, or even making the guests comfortable... Jesus was talking about something, and she was just sat at his feet listening...! I glared at her... I thought about all I'd been doing, how hard I was working, and here she was just sat listening...

Jesus must have seen the look I gave her, for he asked what was wrong... I said to him, "Lord, I'm working really hard to get things ready, whilst Mary here is just sitting doing nothing... Tell her to come and help me." As I spoke I stared at her...

Then I realised that Jesus was saying my name... He said that he wouldn't tell Mary to come because she had chosen what was better and he wasn't going to take that away from her.... "Come, join us," he said...

I thought about the food, Mary, all I'd done, and I looked around me... I knew I had a choice to make... It was hard, I mean, what would you have done?

Monologue based on Luke 15:8-10
The Lost Coin

I was so worried; I was certain that I wasn't going to find it. Sorry, I'm getting ahead of myself, and you're probably wondering what on earth I lost and what I'm talking about! Let me explain.

As is the custom I have a headdress that has upon it ten silver coins as part of my dowry – that is the property I take with me to my husband in marriage. Well, one morning I noticed that one of the coins was missing. I was so upset – how could it have happened?! I thought. There was no way that I could afford to replace it, and how could I marry without it? I began to search the house. Even though it was morning, I lit a lamp so I could see better – our houses have no windows and very low doors, so not much daylight gets in. I looked on the tables and chairs, all the places that I thought it might have been, but just couldn't find it. I was beginning to lose hope, but I knew that I couldn't give up.

I decided to sweep the floor; I did this very carefully, I didn't want to miss the coin if it was there. I decided to work from one end of the room to the other, so that not one place was missed – if the coin was there, I was going to find it! I was looking for ages and began to think that I had lost the coin for ever, and that I'd never get it back, when I saw something catch the light of the lamp, I went straight to it and there it was, right there on the floor. You cannot believe how pleased, how overjoyed I was! I was so happy I called my friends in, told them what had happened and we had a celebration.

A few days later I was telling some other friends what had happened, there were a lot of people around as Jesus was just about to start to teach – but I just had to say what had happened, as I was so pleased! I hadn't realised Jesus was listening, when he started to talk to the people he said, "Suppose a woman has ten silver coins and loses one. Does she not light a lamp, sweep the house and search carefully until she finds it? And when she finds it, she calls her friends and neighbours together and says, 'Rejoice with me, I have found my lost coin.' Then he said, "In the same way the angels of God rejoice over one sinner who repents."

I was speechless – at that moment, I realised just how much I am loved by God, and how much he wanted me to turn to him, to follow him and be his friend. I was desperate to find my lost coin – I learnt that God was even more desperate for me to follow him than I ever was to find that coin, and there was a party in heaven to celebrate my coming to him! Don't you think that's amazing? Oh and he feels the same about you too!

A Monologue: The Prodigal, Seeing Differently.

I thought of myself no better than a servant, no, worse than that: it was as if I were dead. Starving and in rags, I approached my father's lands. I walked slowly, not so much because of my sore feet and weakened body, as fearing the stones hitting me, stones thrown at my father's command, as he drives me from his land and fearing his words as he tells me never to return.

I'd planned a speech; I was going to say that I knew I couldn't be his son and I was going to ask that he take me on as a servant – my pay being shelter and food, which I had been without for so long.

As I approached the edge of his lands, I looked up and saw him running towards me with five, maybe six others.

I stopped and braced myself, readying myself to flee for my life yet knowing I'd be better dead.

As he came closer, I shouted out, hoping to stop his banishment, 'I have sinned against you, father; I don't deserve to be your son but please, father, can I be a servant on your land?'

He just kept coming – as if he hadn't heard. My heart sank. Then I saw him stretch out his arms and say, 'My son. My son!'

'This can't be,' I thought to myself. 'Asking for my inheritance, I was, in effect wishing my father's death. I am not worthy to be a son.'

'A servant,' I said.

'My son,' he said.

I knew I couldn't be a son because I'd wished my father dead, squandered his money, laughed at him, at his folly... but I was the foolish one; I'd wasted everything. No, I'm no son. 'A servant,' I said more weakly.

'My son,' he said again.

I thought that I must have fallen asleep amidst the pigs I fed, that I was delirious in my hunger... but I could feel the warmth of my father's body against my cheek; I could feel his tears and I could hear his voice speaking softly in my ear: 'My son. My son.'

I fell to my knees, 'Father,' I said, and wept.

He held me a long while, then gave orders to those with him – the best robe, a ring, shoes, the fatted calf. 'We will have a feast,' my father said, as he helped me to my feet, 'and you, my son, shall be the honoured guest.'

I'd seen myself as no better than, no, worse than a servant; it was then that I realised that I needed to begin to see myself differently – as a son, as the son I was always meant to be – the son I was born to be.

Monologue: Zacchaeus

I remember the day clearly; there was great excitement throughout the town. We had heard a couple of days before that Jesus was to travel through... I was really excited myself, I'd heard so much of this rabbi, and was looking forward to hearing some of his teaching for myself...

When I got to the road he was travelling on, there were already a great number of people gathered... The day was really hot... dust swirled into the air from the feet of those who had come to see Jesus... Suddenly there was cheering a short distance down the road and I knew Jesus had arrived.... I tried to find my way to the front, because, being short, I couldn't see above the heads of the crowd... It was no good though, once the people saw it was me they shouted at me, "Get away tax-collector..." and they stood more closely together to prevent my seeing Jesus....

By the noise of the crowd I knew Jesus was close... I tried jumping to catch a glimpse of him, but it was no use... all this did was to cause more ridicule, this time from some children who had climbed a tree to see Jesus... They interrupted their cheering and waving to laugh at me and throw figs... as I started to walk away, I looked at the children with sorrow, but it was then that I had the idea...

I looked further along the road and ran to the next tree, a sycamore; this was my chance, my only chance to see Jesus... I climbed the tree and settled myself on a branch... My excitement returned... I could see the crowd moving in my direction, although I couldn't make Jesus out yet... then, suddenly I saw him... It took all I had not to fall out of the tree with excitement... He came closer... it's hard to describe how I felt when Jesus looked to be stopping near the tree... my heart seemed to slow, and I found myself holding my breath... I thought he was going to start teaching, but then he looked up at me... he called me by name, told me to come down, and said that he was going to stay at my house... as I climbed down I wondered if I'd heard correctly, but when I stood at the bottom of the tree Jesus just smiled and indicated that I should lead the way... as we walked he talked to me, asked me questions and listened to me... so many things went through my mind: Why me? What shall we do? What shall I say...?.. I welcomed him into my house... he didn't seem to hear the snide remarks of the crowd as they went on their way, it was as if there was just me and him... I gave him water and later we shared a meal and talked...he made things so easy... it was a long time since someone had listened to me... I listened to him too and as I listened I thought about my life and I knew some things had to change...

I'll never forget that day, the day Jesus came to my house... I'm sure you wouldn't either if it had been you; I mean, how would you react if Jesus invited himself to your house? How would you spend the time...? What would you say...? What would you do...?

Monologue based on the *Woman at the Well*
(John 4)

I can remember it as if it was yesterday. The sand was hot on my feet, and I was weary – but who wouldn't be, working in the midday sun! Back then you see, I didn't go to the well with the other women. They used to talk about me and laugh at me; no one spoke to me apart from throwing insults – I had a name you see; I'd had five husbands, and the man I was living with wasn't one of them... but I'm not going to get into that, that's past... but he knew, Jesus. He knew. He knew before I even told him, and he didn't poke fun at me, or point the finger and make me feel bad.

That's what I was telling you, it was when I was on my way to get water I saw him standing there, by the well. I stopped some distance from the well at first and just looked at him. I mean, he was a man, and a Jew – we Samaritans don't mix with Jews as a rule – but I needed water and the sun was getting hotter...

I decided to just get my water and ignore him. But when I got to the well he spoke to me – not to make fun of me – he asked me for a drink! I thought he was mad – I mean, he didn't have a cup for a start, and like I said, Samaritans and Jews don't mix, and we definitely don't use each others' cups! – I told him as much and then he started talking about Living Water – I didn't understand at first, but then he went on to tell me about myself, and I just knew that he was a man of God. I said to him, "I know the Messiah is coming, and when he comes he will explain everything." "I am he," he said. Something inside welled up like a spring, and I knew it was so... I forgot about the water, the heat of the day, and all the pain and hurt those from my village had caused me and I ran to tell them about the man at the well – "Could this be the Christ?" I asked. They must have seen something different about me because instead of making fun of me as usual they came back to the well with me, they listened to Jesus and many became his followers.

Jesus is the Christ – the one who came to save us. I still find it amazing that he spoke to me, and that he used me to tell others about him...

Monologue: Mary Magdalene – The Resurrection

The Sabbath passed in a daze; since Jesus' crucifixion I'd felt numb – shock I guess... I just couldn't believe what had happened. Jesus dead. Crucified. Crucified like a common criminal, and not only that, but beaten and flogged too... It was horrible... To be honest I just wanted the Sabbath to be over so I could go to my Lord's body and tend it like it ought to have been before that hasty burial; that was the least I could do...

Me and some of the other women bought oils and spices to put on his body. Most of the way we walked in silence, our hearts heavy with grief; I don't know about the others, but I was thinking about what we'd be faced with; I'd seen him on the cross, after the flogging, it made me realise how fragile the body is – his was torn and bleeding, and the worst of it was I could do nothing to comfort him... I couldn't reach him, not to even give him a touch of comfort...

As we walked along, I also kept asking, "Why? Why Jesus?" He who had shown nothing but love – yes, not always an easy-to-accept love, for it could be challenging, difficult, but it was love all the same... And he'd shown this love not only to those deemed acceptable, but to those most used to being shunned, those on the margins, those not thought of as having any significance. Take me for example, once I was like a woman possessed – I didn't know who I was any more. My life couldn't have been any worse; it was a mess. Everyone avoided me, some even showed active contempt and I slid deeper into the pit I was in... I came to Jesus in desperation and despair, half expecting him to shun me too: to tell me to "Get out!" Instead, he looked at me with love; then he reached out and healed me... I don't think I'd been touched out of love before... that touch was the beginning of the rebuilding of my life... I owed him everything... And now I was walking to his grave...

As I wondered about these things one of the others said, "How will we move the stone away?" To be honest I hadn't thought of that, I just knew I needed to do this one thing for Jesus, who had given me so much; we'd never move the stone on our own. After all he'd done for me, and I wasn't even going to be able to do this simple thing for him... None of it seemed real... Why was this happening?

We just kept going: our hearts even heavier, if that were possible! We hoped that there would be someone around to move the stone for us, yet at the same time, doubted there would be...

When the grave came in sight, we couldn't believe our eyes, there was no stone over the entrance, someone had got there before us, and had moved it... We hurried forward and cautiously looked in, but the grave was empty... the grave clothes were there, but Jesus' body wasn't... My heart sank, I felt angry too; who would do this? Hadn't they done enough? Couldn't they give him the dignity in death they had denied him in life? ... We just looked at each other, at a loss as to what to do... crying... Suddenly, there were, what I can only describe as two men in bright shining clothes standing there. We bowed in fear, and they said, "Why do you look for the living among the dead? He is not here, he is risen!" Then they reminded us that Jesus had said it would be so, that he would die, then rise again – I couldn't catch my breath, I could hardly believe it, but I did believe it and my sorrow turned to laughter and my tears to joy...

Monologue: Road To Emmaus

We'd decided to go back to our home village – what else could we do? As we walked along we talked, picking over the events of the last few days: Jesus' trial, the flogging, the crucifixion and then, just that morning the women coming and saying that Jesus wasn't dead after all, but alive – ah! They'd said that they'd been told this by angels no less, couldn't believe it myself – I just thought, "No way, I saw his broken body, I saw him hanging there, and the spear go into his side"; Cleopas was of the same mind so we both decided to go on with our plans to go home, I mean I'm no doctor, but I'm no fool either – well, I thought I wasn't...

Anyway, there we were, talking over events, not really in any rush – I mean, the one that gave meaning to our lives was dead – it was like having all your dreams irreparably shattered... I found myself wondering, "What's the point?" So we walked and talked. Cleopas is good like that, I can be honest with him, tell him my disappointment, my shattered dreams, anyway, there we were and this guy just came and started walking beside us. Gave me a bit of a start actually, I hadn't realised that there was someone behind us. He was all smiles greeted us like long lost brothers – made me a bit irritable, especially when he said or should I say shouted, "Why so glum looking?!" I couldn't believe it.

Cleopas took the words out of my mouth (well, actually, he put it much nicer than I would have!) and said, "Are you a visitor to Jerusalem? Do you not know what's happened these past few days?" "What things?" came the reply, so we told him about Jesus, his life, the hope we had in him, his arrest, and death, then we told him about what the women had said that morning...

And what did he say? Only called us foolish! Before I could open my mouth to protest he began to explain about the scriptures, and what it says about the Christ – the prophecies and everything... something about him needing to suffer, I didn't really understand fully then, but I did realise that my irritation ebbed away, and, looking back so did my grief, to some extent... I thought I knew the scriptures pretty well, but this man seemed to bring new meaning, I can't tell you what it was, but I just wanted more, so when we reached Emmaus, we invited him to stay with us, it was getting dark after all... He agreed and we asked him to tell us more...

When we got home we sat down to share a simple meal. Before eating he took the bread and gave thanks to God, then broke it and reached over to give it to us – I was stunned, just in those words, that movement... How could I have been so blind? ... Jesus. It was Jesus. I looked at Cleopas and I knew that he had seen it too... then Jesus was gone... but nothing could take away the burning in my heart, the excitement, the new life I felt – Jesus was alive, he had risen from the dead, he was, is alive...

Meditation based on Luke 2:1, 3-7
Journey to Bethlehem and The Nativity

Caesar Augustus issued a decree that a census should be taken of the entire Roman world... And everyone went to his own town to register. So Joseph also went up from the town of Nazareth in Galilee to Judea, to Bethlehem the town of David, because he belonged to the house and line of David. He went there to register with Mary, who was pledged to be married to him and was expecting a child. While they were there, the time came for the baby to be born, and she gave birth to her firstborn, a son. She wrapped him in cloths and placed him in a manger, because there was no room for them at the inn.

Imagine yourself travelling alongside Mary and Joseph as they travel towards Bethlehem, the destination of their long journey... Take in the scenery, the hills, trees dotted here and there... feel the cold winter wind on your face... notice the sound as you travel towards your destination... Look at Joseph and Mary... What do they look like to you? ...Notice Mary, heavily pregnant, tired after such a long journey...

As you imagine yourself there with Mary and Joseph, do you notice any others travelling with you, others also walking to the town of David to register in the census?

Where are you in the scene that you see? What is your part? Are you watching from a distance, or are you beside them?

...Are Mary and Joseph travelling in silence... or are they talking to each other, to others, or to you? ... Are you walking in silence, or are you speaking? Do you want to speak? If so, what do you want to say?...

As you journey closer to Bethlehem, take in the changing sights and sounds... people seem to be everywhere... some are shouting, calling to anyone who will listen as they try to sell their goods: you take in the scent of different foods, you see different coloured cloths for sale, animals wandering around, birds in cages... everywhere there are people: men, women and children, all pushing, and rushing to find a place to stay before nightfall... Look at Mary and Joseph as they also walk through these crowds, searching for a place to rest...

Be with them as they find an inn and ask for a room, only to be told the inn is full... Look at their faces, Mary arms protecting her unborn child... Joseph, worried, and wondering what to do... Journey with them as they go from one inn to another only to be turned away again and again...

It becomes evident that Mary has gone into labour... yet they continue to be turned away... Look at their faces as they continue to search for a room, with, it seems, little hope of finding one... be aware of what you are thinking and feeling... Do you want to say anything? Who do you want to speak to? What do you want to say? ...

Look at their faces as when at last they are offered shelter, not in a warm room in an inn, but in a stable... you walk into the stable with them... look around, what do you see? Listen... smell the smells of the stable...

Mary by now is having regular contractions and she cries out in pain... Joseph prepares a place for her and the coming child on the floor of the stable... where are you? ... Are you watching from a distance, or are you active in the preparations? ... How is the labour going...? Mary cries out again... Look at her face... and at Joseph... What do you see?

What do you think and what do you feel as you watch as Mary struggles in the latter stages of labour and the baby's head begins to appear? ...

You watch as the baby is born... He takes his first breath and cries... Watch as he is comforted, wiped clean... wrapped in cloths... suckles at the breast ... notice how you feel as you watch this...

Imagine Mary handing him to you... or imagine sitting beside him as he lays in the fresh straw of the manger... gaze at him... and, if you wish to, speak to him...

As he drifts into a restful sleep, and Mary and Joseph also rest... think through the day's events... your experiences... your thoughts... feeling... fears and hopes...

And if you wish to, share them with the Christ child, who is God with us...

Meditation on Matthew 2:1, 9a–11
The Visit of the Magi

Imagine that you are travelling with others; it is winter, and dark... The wind blows cold against your skin, and you pull your cloak closer... You've been travelling for many weeks, as your back, legs and feet can testify... You are not sure where you are heading, as you are not sure where the star that is leading you will stop... You look at that star now... You wonder about it as you remember the things that you heard the men you travel with say about it... You look at these men, their fine dress, and camels... You walk alongside them your head bent against the wind, thinking about the last few days.

You had thought that you had reached your destination back in Jerusalem... you remember how you'd no sooner begun to relax when you were off again... just when you were getting used to the place, you had to leave... now it was dark again, cold and you long for the rough bed you had found in Jerusalem, just to warm and rest your body. You wonder why Jerusalem wasn't the place; as you walk, you listen, as best you can, as the men beside you talk ...

Suddenly you hear a change in their tone: excitement as they realise that at last the star has stopped, and you look to see where it has led you... Eventually you come to the place, your journey is over... notice how you feel... you watch as the men you have travelled with take gifts from their bags, and enter the place where the star has led them... Notice how you feel as you see these important men, who had first gone to a great palace, now enter a humble home... notice your reaction as you see them kneel and bow their heads to a tiny child... Take in the scene, the surroundings, the parents, the child... What does it look like, smell like, feel like? Listen as the men give their praise... Watch as they offer their gifts... You hear the gold clinking together... you smell the frankincense and the myrrh and wonder at these strange gifts for a child...

Then you notice the child's mother stretching out her hand and beckoning to you to come forward... You hesitate... But she smiles and continues to beckon you forward... You move forward, and she shows you the child... You look at him and talk to him...

Meditation on Mark 8:22-26
The Healing of a Blind Man at Bethsaida

As you sit with your eyes closed, become aware of what you are noticing with your other senses – smell, hearing, touch, as you do this, relax and enjoy what you are experiencing... now become aware of the darkness... try to imagine that you are in the time of Jesus and have been blind since birth...

You feel the hot sun beating down on you. You are being hastily led by a group of friends. You hear the excited and yet anxious voices as they tell you of Jesus' arrival. As they carry you along you taste the disturbed dust that fills the air with each step... you recognise friends by their distinctive smell, and feel the anxious, eager hands holding you just a little too tightly... Suddenly you are brought to a standstill and you hear the familiar voices of your friends begging Jesus to touch you, to heal you...

The eager, friendly hands that held you now let go. You hear as they make way for Jesus to come to you... you hear his footsteps in the silence... you sense him stop close to you... Jesus takes your hand... he leads you away until you are alone with him – away from the crowd... you feel anxious, yet trust this stranger...

You hear a noise and moments later feel the cold moisture of Jesus' spit hit your unseeing eyes... then you feel Jesus' hands touching you and hear his fingers move across your skin... "Do you see anything?" he asks... apprehensively you open your eyes... the cold darkness is gone, but things are still not clear... tell Jesus what you see...

You stay close to Jesus... closing your eyes again, you feel Jesus touch your eyes a second time; you hear his fingers move across your skin... once again you open your eyes... you see Jesus clearly now, and you talk to him...

Meditation on Mark 8:27-29
Who do you say I am?

Picture yourself walking along with a group of others. Feel the heat of the sun on your skin. Taste the dryness of your mouth on this hot day, and see the dust that is unsettled as you walk along. Notice how you feel.

Look at those around you – Jesus, the disciples, and other followers of Jesus... listen to the conversation about Jesus' latest healing miracle – the healing of a blind man... Listen to what is said... look at the faces of those with you... notice how you feel... notice what you are thinking... do you want to say anything? What do you want to say?...

There is laughter and discussion as you walk along, then Jesus asks, "Who do the people say I am?" The laughter stops, as this question is taken in... How do you feel?... You hear someone answer, "I've heard people say that you are John the Baptist come back to life..." You notice your reaction to this; then another disciple says to Jesus, "Well, I've heard you called Elijah by some, and others say you are one of the other prophets..."

Jesus says to the whole group with him, "And what about you? Who do you say I am?" You notice the reactions of others... some are looking at the floor... some begin to walk on ... others look at each other, not knowing what to say... not wanting to 'get it wrong'... Notice how you feel... Notice your thoughts... Then a voice says, "You are the Christ!" You turn and see Peter's smiling face... Jesus looks at each person in turn... Notice how you are feeling...

Jesus' gaze rests on you; he looks into your eyes and asks, "What about you? Who do you say I am?

Seeing Jesus' Glory
Mark 9:2-8

Imagine that you are walking up the side of a mountain... Jesus leads the way, you hear the crunch of the ground as you walk... the sun is shining, the sun and the effort of the walk is making you hot and you feel the sweat on your brow... every so often, there is a cool breeze, which you welcome and find refreshing. You lick your lips in a bid to lessen the feeling of thirst; you hear the sound of your breath get louder with the effort...

You eventually reach the top and Jesus stops... you take out your water bottle and take a drink of the cool liquid, feel it slide down your throat into your belly... then you turn and look at the view, taking in the village below, the houses, the trees, the people who just look like ants; you see the distant hills and the haze caused by the sun... as your breathing returns to normal you notice the quietness of the place... you hear a bird sing... the sound of the gentle wind blowing... you and your companion sit on the ground, smiling at the beauty of what you see and hear... look around at the scene, notice as you do, how you feel...

You look at Jesus and wonder why he has brought you to this place... as you look at him, he seems to change before your eyes, you see him differently... it is as if he has become like light, his clothes are brilliant white... you rub your eyes, thinking it a trick of the light... then you look again and you notice two others with Jesus... you want to look, yet also cover your eyes, unable to look... notice how you feel...

You are impelled to look again and see a cloud descend over Jesus and the two with him... then you hear a voice... your heart begins to race, you close your eyes and cover your ears with your hands but you hear clearly, 'This is my son, whom I love. Listen to him'...notice how you feel as you hear the words...

Then all seems to be still again and you lower your arms and open your eyes... you see Jesus smiling at you and the words echo in your head, 'This is my son, whom I love. Listen to him.'... 'Listen to him.'...

Sit with Jesus for a while, talk to him about how you feel, about what you saw, your understanding of who he is and listen to him...

Meditation on Mark 10:46-51 / Luke 18:35-43
Bartimaeus Receives Sight

Imagine you are sitting on the side of the road; the sun is hot and bright, but you are in darkness, blind from birth you sit by the road seeking money and food from passers-by. You hear sounds of people coming and going, and the voices of those around you; you taste the dust which is disturbed as people walk past, and which floats on a gentle breeze, which periodically brings relief from the hot sun. It seems like any other day.

Then you sense a change in the people around you, and more people begin to line the road, something seems to be happening, but your sightless eyes fail to see what... You call out, "What is it? What's happening?" At first nobody answers so you call again, "What's happening?"

"It's Jesus" someone says, "Jesus of Nazareth; he's coming this way."

Notice how you feel about this news – Jesus 'coming this way', right past where you are. You've heard of this Jesus, his teachings and the healing he has done...

Sensing that Jesus is coming closer you begin to call out, "Jesus of Nazareth; Jesus, son of David, have mercy on me!" Those around you push you and tell you to be quiet; they move closer together and push you out, blocking your way to Jesus...

But you shout louder, "Jesus of Nazareth; Jesus, son of David, have mercy on me!" From the sound of the crowd you sense that Jesus is close. You continue to ignore the calls for you to be quiet and call out over and over, "Jesus of Nazareth; Jesus, son of David, have mercy on me!"

Then the crowd fall quiet and there is a moment's silence before someone grabs your arm and says, "Come on, on your feet! He's calling you!" Feelings flood in as you realise that you have been heard... those who had moments earlier been pushing you out and telling you to be quiet now separated to make a way for you to approach Jesus... Leaving the few belongings you have, you follow eagerly and with haste as you are led to where Jesus waits for you...

As you reach Jesus your guide lets go of your arm, all are quiet, and although you know there are many people around, it feels as though there is just you and him: you and Jesus. Then Jesus speaks and asks, "What do you want me to do for you?"

Answer him in your own way.

A Meditation
Based on the Parable of the
Wise and Foolish Virgins
(Matthew 25:1-13)

Imagine yourself sitting on a grassy bank under the shade of a sycamore tree. The sun is warm but not hot and a cool breeze catches your cheek every now and again... You are sitting with your back to the trunk of the tree and you feel the pattern of the bark through your clothes... There are others with you and still more arriving: you greet them and make room for them.... There is easy, friendly chatter all around... you note how you are feeling...

A few feet away sits Jesus, who looks straight at you and begins to speak, as he does so, everyone else falls silent and listens... you listen too... he begins to tell a story... "You know," he says, "how the bridesmaids prepare the bride to meet her groom and process her through the streets with lit torches from her family home to his family home?"

"Well, there were ten such bridesmaids, each with their long pole and rag torches..." You close your eyes and imagine the scene in your mind's eye, as he continues with his story...

"Five bridesmaids had lots of spare oil and five had none... As always with these celebrations, there was a lot of preparation and the bridegroom was late... as the daylight faded and darkness fell, the bridesmaids became sleepy and they all fell asleep..."

"At midnight the cry went out that the bridegroom was about to arrive... the bridesmaids woke and shook themselves into action... those who had oil, trimmed the charred rags and poured new oil on them, giving fresh flame to them.... Those without oil asked to use some of that of the other bridesmaids but were refused because there wasn't enough; instead they were told to go and buy oil for themselves, which is what they did...."

Knowing that this wasn't a good thing for the bridesmaids and eager to hear what happened, you open your eyes and, watching Jesus, wait for the ending of the story... again he looks at you.... It is as if he is speaking only to you.... "What happened?" someone called out.... your gaze remains on Jesus.... and his on you...

"The five went off to buy oil," Jesus said, "but while they were gone, the bridegroom arrived and the procession went on without them... by the time they came back, the bride, bridegroom and everyone else, were in the banquet already and the unprepared bridesmaids were denied entrance to the festivities..."

Those around you begin to discuss the story amongst themselves... then you notice Jesus has come and crouched in front of you... You have a conversation about the story.... you talk to him about what it means to you and how you feel about it, you place yourself in the story... you imagine taking the different parts, each in a time of waiting, and you talk to Jesus about how you feel...

You talk to Jesus about where in the story you feel most comfortable... you don't judge yourself, you simply say how it is...

and you listen to his response...

A Meditation based on John 13:
Washing of the Disciples' Feet

Imagine that you sitting at a table sharing a meal with a number of others... Jesus is there, his disciples and followers... notice where you are in the room... what can you hear, what are people talking about – maybe Jesus' triumphal entry into Jerusalem, or maybe how Jesus had spoken about his death, or something else... use all your senses to explore the scene that you are in, and notice how you feel...

Then you notice Jesus get up and take off his coat and tie a towel around his waist... You watch what he is doing... notice how you feel as he takes a bowl of water and kneels at the feet of one of his disciples... take in his movement, and the reaction of the disciple and the others in the room as they realise what's happening... hear the water as he uses it to wash the feet of his disciple... notice how you are feeling... Watch as Jesus stands and moves to the next person, kneels and washes their feet... see him touch the feet, holding them, using the water to clean them, then the towel to dry them... notice how you feel as he draws closer to you... now it is your turn, Jesus comes to you, you look at him and he says, "Let me wash your feet"... notice how you are feeling, what will your reaction be...

Allow the scene to unfold wherever it leads... Talk to Jesus about what you are thinking and how you feel... Silence...

Meditation on a Sunflower Seed

Traditionally Jews in the west face east when praying – towards Jerusalem, or rather towards the place the Temple once stood. Traditionally Churches also faced east, towards Jerusalem, the place where God most fully revealed himself in Jesus Christ.

Sunflowers follow the path of the sun as they grow, then once their flower is fully out, they too face east – this meditation is based on these two facts: the tradition of facing east while praying and the movement of the sunflower.

Ensure everyone is holding a sunflower seed.

Spend some time quietening and relaxing.

The meditation:

As you hold the sunflower seed in your hand, look at the shape of it, its colour, its size... Think about the potential within that small seed; think about the life it holds within it...

Imagine the journey the seed you hold might take, you might like to close your eyes while still holding your seed.

Imagine burying the seed in the darkness of soil... keeping it watered and in sunlight... Imagine after several weeks a tiny green shoot pushing through the soil...

You watch as over time this tiny plant grows in strength and height... as you watch you notice a small bud forming... you take in its movement through the day... and realise that it is following the path of the sun, even on days when the sun is weak the plant turns towards it, seeking its touch, its heat, its strength, its life... Seeking all the time the gaze of the sun... Then the day comes when the flower head begins to open and there is a glorious display of colour...

You look at the flower in admiration at different times through the day and realise that the flower has stopped chasing the sun, but is now simply basking in its heat and constantly facing east....

Think about the journey of the sunflower and relate it to your own journey... have there been times when you've felt buried in darkness... times when God has felt very far away...

Now remember, if you can, times when you have felt as though you have broken through into Sunlight – into the Light of the Son... Remember what that felt like, meeting with God... feeling His touch... hearing His Word... (Maybe this was through the word of a friend, through music, or seeing a beautiful scene...)

Think about the bud of the sunflower faithfully following the path of the sun and think about your own journey of following Jesus, the Son... Reflect on how you feel about it...

Think about where you are in your journey now... From where do you get your strength? Who or what do you seek to give you life, to touch your heart, and how do you do this? Think of the bud of the sunflower, faithfully following the path of the sun... and think of your own following of Jesus the Son...

Now remember the open flower, constantly facing east... towards the place God the Father revealed himself most fully... think about where you yourself are facing in your spiritual life, are you happy there, or is there a desire to face a different direction?... The sunflower freely rests in the heat of the sun, imagine yourself resting in Jesus the Son...

God's seed is in each one of us, imagine God's seed in you facing the Son, Jesus, and that seed being woken from sleep, growing in strength and height, following the Son, until you feel able to rest in the warm touch of the Son, facing God the Father...

Talk to God about anything you feel you need to...

Try & Try Again: A Meditation

Relax.

Imagine yourself sitting in a chair. In your hand you have a walking stick; as you look at it you begin to think over the past months...

You remember the day that you woke to find yourself in a strange bed and a strange room. You tried to get up, but found that you couldn't... then a hand touched yours and a voice said, "It's okay, just lie still..." You turned to see someone you knew, a friend... it was they who told you what had happened and how you had come to be in hospital...

You remember the beginning of the physiotherapy – at first the physiotherapists had to move your legs for you... they were always gentle, and always cheerful... sometimes you just wanted to tell them to leave you alone and take their cheer elsewhere... you would lie in bed willing your legs to move but in your frustration nothing happened and you grew more angry and fearful...the physiotherapy exercises and the pain they caused you were exhausting, and you often wondered if it would ever end... it went on and on... regularly each day they would come; over and over again the exercises were done... sometimes it wasn't so bad, but other times you couldn't wait for it to end... and there was that time when you absolutely refused to let them near you, holding the bed clothes tight...

It was soon after that when that nursing sister spoke to you... asked you how you felt... you told of your humiliation, your frustration and your fears, and for the first time you cried... And there were many tears after this too – tears of grief, tears of frustration and anger... and out of frustration, anger and grief, sometimes you shouted at those who came to visit or those caring for you... yet they continued to be there for you...

The physiotherapy continued, and you began to feel the difference – you gained more control of your legs...then one day the physiotherapists said that it was time to get up... it was strange, because although this is what you had been waiting for, now it was here you feared it... silently you argued against them... but you followed their instructions, and with their help you stood and shuffled to a nearby chair... a victory!!

The physiotherapy continued it was slow and tiring, and sometimes painful: you began walking with aid on both sides... then went onto using a walking frame... you noticed the difference more now... yet it was still frustrating watching people doing things for you that once you could do on your own and there was a couple of times you tried to run ahead and found yourself helplessly lying on the floor...

Each step was like a victory won... a battle over come... You noticed that one leg dragged a little, and wasn't as strong as it had been in the past... with the help of the physiotherapists you found a new way of walking to accommodate the lost power...

Then you remember you were given two walking sticks... another victory... another hurdle overcome... the exercises continued, and were tiring, but didn't exhaust you like they had in the past... then one day you found yourself pottering around your room with one stick, with the other hand free... and now you are sitting in your room, in your chair, looking at your walking stick, waiting to be taken home... you know that at home there will be new challenges to overcome... you know that the work of recovery isn't finished yet...

You make your way to the door and close it behind you...

Talk to God about your experience in this time of meditation.

You may like to share any feelings you have of struggling in your life and ask:

Are their things in your spiritual life that you finding difficult at the moment?

Have there been times when you have struggled, persevered and come through – what made a difference? What kept you going?

What do you need now?

Written by the same author

A Hope and A Future is a collection of poems and illustrations by Adelaide Morley, born our of her expereince with depression. It was published in 2004 and the ISBN number is: 1-904446-05-1 Four poems from that book can be found on the following pages: '*Don't Dismiss Me, Please*', '*Silently Eating*', '*You are Here*' and '*Images of God*'. (All are © A.W. Morley)

Don't Dismiss Me, Please

Please don't be quick
To conclude about who I am.
Please don't dismiss me as
Unloving and uncaring.

Please do not label me,
And dismiss me as
"Moody", "unpredictable",
"Unreliable, or "weird".

Please take time to know me.
To look a little deeper.
Please try to look beyond
My fortress exterior:

See the pain inside
Which holds the walls in place.
See the hear, so full of love,
In a shadow: afraid to shine.

See my arms stretched out
To be taken by another's.
Hear my cry: a cry for love:
Afraid to call, or to receive.

Prease don't be quick
To conclude or dismiss,
Take time to win my trust:
Help me take down the bricks.

Please don't be quick
To conclude about who I am.
Please don't dismiss me;
Help me, and let us learn together,

The truth of who I am.

Silently Eating

Silently eating,
You hurt because
Of a lack of words,
Inside I'm struggling,
"What can I say?"
Always the same,
Fear disables.

Those I know are
Easy, strangers
Created fear, panic,
Vulnerability.
My silence is not
Your disability,
It is mine.

You are Here

I came looking for you,
Only to find that you weren't missing.
I listened for you in the silence,
Not hearing your constant wooing of my soul.
I ached to feel your touch,
Not realizing you held me in your hand.
I came looking for you,
And found that you are, and always have been here.

Images of God

I kept you in a box,
Unwilling to look at you, or myself.
I feared your reproach, your anger, your rejection.
Then you saw me falter and turn
You ran to me.
And in my weakness helped me to open the lid long closed.

An exposion of colour burst forth;
I stepped back – amazed and in awe.
You smiled and drew me closer.
Gently, slowly, you guided me –
You know my fears;
You opened yourself up to me,
Being sensitive to what I could bear,
Using mediuns you knew I felt safe with,
And could understand.

You showed me your love through the love of another,
You taught me of your care through the vains of the leaves,
Your provision I learned through hard times,
And our power through the flight of a seagull.
The fragrance of flowers spoke to me of your gentleness,
And recently a pebble spoke to me of your love.

But there still remains so much to learn, to live, to expereince.
Sometimes the fear of you is again intense,
Other times I seek and cannot find you –
Where are you then, O God?

In these times, helpf me to remember the pebble,
    the leaves, the easgull, the flower,
Or lead me to a new image that will tell me of you,
And lead me to have life to the full.